The Way

Student's Book

Book 1

The Way, the Truth and the Life series
Religious Education series for 11 to 14 year olds

Key Stage 3

by P. J. McHugh

CATHOLIC TRUTH SOCIETY

PUBLISHERS TO THE HOLY SEE

Nihil obstat: Father Anton Cowan (Censor)
Imprimatur: Monsignor Thomas Egan, V.G., Westminster, 22 March 2000
The Nihil obstat and Imprimatur *are a declaration that the book or pamphlet is considered to be free from doctrinal or moral error. It is not implied that those who have granted the* Nihil obstat *and* Imprimatur *agree with the contents, opinions or statements expressed.*

Published 2000 by The Incorporated Catholic Truth Society, 40-46 Harleyford Road, London SE11 5AY
Tel: 020 7640 0042 Fax: 020 7640 0046

ISBN: 186082 083 2 CTS Code: Ed 05

Designed and Produced by: The Catholic Truth Society/ Stephen Campbell.

Front Cover: *The Sermon on the Mount,* Fra Angelico, courtesy of AKG London; cover photographs courtesy of PA Photos/EPA.

Illustrations: © Philip Hood/ Arena, unless stated below. Lucy Scherer/ Arena, illustrator's agent.

Photography: © Carlos Reyes-Manzo/ Andes Press Agency, unless stated below. Val Baker/ Andes Press Agency, photography co-ordination.

Printed by: The GreenShires Group Limited.

The publisher acknowledges permission to reproduce the following:- *Page 7*: Folio from St. John's Gospel, Greek codex of the Bible, 4th century. Facsimile published by the Claredon Press, Oxford, vol. 1. New Testament 1911. Original manuscript in the British Library Codex Sinaiticus Bible Society, London, UK/Bridgeman Art Library. *Page 10*: The Torah is prepared for Shabbat celebrations. PA PHOTOS/EPA. *Page 10*: Sheet from a Koran (Qur'an) manuscript in Kufic script. Bibliothèque Nationale, Tunis. Photo: AKG London/Jean-Louis Nou. *Page 13*: Catholic pilgrims in Paris. PA PHOTOS/EPA. *Page 14*: A (1526) edition of William Tyndale's New Testament. Now held in the British Library. PA PHOTOS/EPA. *Page 14*: St. Francis of Assisi (c. 1182-1226) from "Sunday Sunshine", pub. John Shaw and Co., London, 1920's (book illustration) by English School (20th Century). Private collection/Bridgeman Art Library. *Page 15*: "The Burning Thornbush" (Exodus 3, 1-12) by Merian, Matthäus the elder. Photo: AKG London. *Page 16*: Image courtesy of PhotoDisc Europe Ltd. *Page 18*: Jesus Washing Peter's Feet, 1876 by Ford Madox Brown (1821-93). Manchester City Art Galleries, UK/Bridgeman Art Library. *Page 18*: Jesus carrying the Cross by Sebastiano del Piombo (S. Luciani) (c. 1485-1547). Prado, Madrid, Spain/Bridgeman Art Library. *Page 18*: The Resurrection, c. 1463 (fresco) by Piero della Francesca (c. 1419/21-92). Pinacoteca, Sansepolcro, Italy/Bridgeman Art Library. *Page 20*: Image courtesy of PhotoDisc Europe Ltd. *Page 23*: Devotees in prayer at World Moslem Congregation in Tongi. PA PHOTOS/EPA. *Page 23*: Santiago de Compostela, Cathedral (Spain). Portal of Glory. Photo: AKG London/G. Mermet. *Page 26*: Illustrations © Stephen Campbell. *Page 27*: A boy lights a candle. PA PHOTOS/EPA. *Page 28*: Sermon on the Mount, Fra Angelico. Photo: AKG London. *Page 37*: Magnificat, 1909 by Maurice Denis (1870- 1943) Private Collection/ Peter Willi/ Bridgeman Art Library. *Page 39*: A mourner holds rosary beads. PA PHOTOS/EPA. *Page 41*: Greenshires Print Group. *Page 41*: Detail of a Russian icon, 19th century. Private collection, Frankfurt. Photo: AKG London. *Page 45*: The Expulsion from Paradise, Masaccio, 1401-1428. Capella Brancacci, Florence. Photo: AKG London/E. Lessing. *Page 55*: The Light of the World by William Holman Hunt (1827-1910). Keble College, Oxford, UK/Bridgeman Art Library. *Page 58*: Aerial photographs taken of Turkey and Mozambique. PA PHOTOS/EPA. *Page 60*: Privatarchiv Jägerstätter Radegund. Courtest of Pat Gaffney, Pax Christi. *Page 67*: The Tax Collector by Marinus van Roejmerswaelen (c. 1493-1567). Musée de Beaux-Arts, Valenciennes, France/Giraudon/Bridgeman Art Library. *Page 67*: The Return of the Prodigal Son, 1823 (oil on canvas) by S. M. Stapleaux (1799-1881) J-L (1748-1825), Private Collection/Bridgeman Art Library. *Page 69*: "Le Fils Prodigue" (The Prodigal Son) 1975-76. Marc Chagall (1887-1985), Private collection. Photo: AKG London. *Page 71*: The Calling of St. Peter and St. Andrew, illustration for 'The Life of Christ', c. 1886-94 (gouache on paper) by James Jacques Joseph Tissot (1836-1902). Brooklyn Museum of Art, New York, USA/Bridgeman Art Library. *Page 72*: A crowd in Bucharest, Romania. PA PHOTOS/EPA. *Page 73-74*: Details of The Last Supper, 1648 (oil on canvas) by Philippe de Champaigne (1602-74). Louvre, Paris, France/Bridgeman Art Library. *Page 75*: Appointment of the Apostles Peter and Andrew, Illuminated manuscript on parchment, Fra Angelico, 1387-1455. Museo di san Marco, Florence. Photo: AKG London/Orsi Battaglini. *Page 78*: The Apostle Simon (Peter) by Peter Paul Rubens (1577-1640). Prado, Madrid, Spain/Bridgeman Art Library. *Page 80*: St. Peter Visited in Jail by St. Paul, c. 1480 (fresco) by Filippino Lippi (c. 1457-1504). Brancacci Chapel, santa Maria del Carmine, Florence, Italy/ Bridgeman Art Library. *Page 84*: The Crucifixion of St. Peter. Filippino Lippi, (c. 1457-1504). Cappella Brancacci, Florence. Photo: AKG London/S. Domingi. *Page 84*: Collage: Portrait of Pope Leo XIII, Vincenzo Gioacchino Pecci (1810-1903), popr from 1878. (oil on canvas) by Theodor Breidwiser ot Breitwieser (b. 1847). Lobkowicz Collections, Nelahozeves Castle, Czech Republic/Bridgeman Art Library. Pope Julius II (oil on panel) by Raphael (Raffaello Sanzio of Urbino) (1483-1520). National Gallery, London, UK/Bridgeman Art Library. Portrait of Pope Benedict XV by Antonio Maria Fabres y Costa (b. 1854). Museo del Prado (Cason del Buen Retiro), Madrid, Spain/Bridgeman Art Library. *Page 90*: St. Peter healing a cripple, and the raising of Tabitha, c. 1427 (fresco) by Tommaso Masolino (1383-1447). Brancacci Chapel, Santa Maria del Carmine, Florence, Italy/Bridgeman art Library. *Page 100*: A detail of The Last Judgement (panel) by Fr Angelico (Guido di Pietro), (c. 1387-1455). Palazzo Barberini, Rome, Italy/Roger-Viollet, Paris Bridgeman Art Library. (For those images for which we have been unable to trace the copyright holder, the Publisher would be grateful to receive any information as to their identity).

Introduction

Welcome to *'The Way, the Truth and the Life'* series.

A word first of all about the title. It is Jesus who said: 'I am the Way, the Truth and the Life' *(John 14:6)*. I would like you to think deeply about what this means for you.

As you progress through your RE lessons in Key Stage 3 I hope you will come to a deeper knowledge, understanding and love of the Word of God as revealed to us in the Scriptures and the teaching of the Church.

This book is going to show you the Way. The contents are challenging, but through a study of the Bible, Prayer, Advent, Sacraments and the Church I hope that you will come to understand much more about the invitation Our Lord is extending to you.

I hope, too, that you will respond generously to His invitation, in faith and love.

✠ Vincent Nichols
Bishop in North London, February 2000.

Contents

Contents

Acknowledgements

Considerable thanks are due to all the RE teachers of the secondary schools in the north and east areas of the Westminster Archdiocese who contributed to this Student's Book by way of advice, editorial review and comment. *'The Way, the Truth and the Life'* series for Key Stage 3 Religious Education has been a collaborative exercise from start to finish. Kind thanks are expressed in particular to the following schools:

(East area, Westminster Archdiocese:)
Bishop Challoner RC School, Tower Hamlets.
Blessed John Roche RC School, Tower Hamlets.
Cardinal Pole RC School, Hackney.
La Sainte Union Convent School, Camden.
Mount Carmel RC School, Islington.
Maria Fidelis Convent School, Camden.
Our Lady's Convent School, Hackney.
St. Aloysius College, Islington.

(North area, Westminster Archdiocese)
Bishop Douglas RC School, Barnet.

Cardinal Hinsley RC High School, Brent.
Convent of Jesus & Mary Language College, Brent.
Finchley Catholic High School, Barnet.
St. Gregory's RC School, Brent.
St. Michael's Grammar School, Barnet.
St. Anne's RC School, Enfield.
St. James' RC High School, Barnet.
St. Thomas More RC School, Haringey.
St. Martha's Convent School, Barnet.
Salvatorian College, Harrow.
St. Ignatius College, Enfield.
Sacred Heart RC School, Harrow.

Sr. Marcellina Cooney, CP, Secondary RE Adviser of the north and east areas of Westminster Archdiocese has co-ordinated this project throughout, and Rt. Rev. Vincent Nichols, as Bishop in North London, supported and encouraged this project since its earliest beginnings.

The supporting website http://www.tere.org was set up thanks to the partnership between Mount Carmel Roman Catholic School for Girls (London Borough of Islington) and City and Islington College. Design was by Tamarin Design Ltd.

Worksheets have been developed in conjunction with this Student's Book for classroom use, and are to be found in the companion Teacher's Book. Schools using this Student's Book should also take full advantage of the Teacher's Book and the supporting website.

******

On a more personal note, I would also like to thank other Heads of RE who provided invaluable support and feedback on the material: Patrick Harrison, Paul Hughes, Hugh Walters and Greg Baines. I offer my thanks also to the Catholic Truth Society for seeing this book through to final publication and to the Assumptionist Community in Burnt Oak for their generous support. A particular debt of gratitude is owed to Kevin and Christy Fitzpatrick and to Anita Parkin for advice and moral support at vital stages of this project.

P. J. McHugh, March 2000

1 The Word of God

What is the Bible?

The world's largest library has over twenty million books. For Christians one book out of all these books is special, set apart - in other words, *holy*. Christians believe this book to be the Word of God. This book is called the *Bible*.

Some facts about the Bible

Bible means 'book' or 'books'. Some have said that more people in history have read some part of the Bible than any other book. It has been translated into about 2,000 languages.

Christians believe the Bible to be the **Word of God**. God gradually showed what he is really like through his Word. This is called *revelation*.

God spoke through human writers. God's Spirit, the Holy Spirit, guided them as they wrote. This is called *inspiration*.

The Bible is made up of many books; the Catholic Church counts 72 books in all. These are split into the **Old Testament** and the **New Testament**.

The **Old Testament** contains 45 books; they are about God and Israel before the time of Jesus. These Books were written mostly in Hebrew, יהוה, a language spoken by Israeli people today. Jews (and Christians) consider these Hebrew books to be holy.

The **New Testament** has 27 books; it is the story of how God became man in Jesus; it also is the story of Jesus' followers and of the Church. These books were written in Greek, ΚΥΡΙΟΣ, which was a language many peoples knew at the time of Jesus.

A photograph of the one of the earliest copies of St. John's Gospel.

Activities

1. Read again the facts about the Bible. Copy and complete the passage below.

Christians believe the ⬚ to be the ⬚ of ⬚. The writers of the Bible were guided by the ⬚ ⬚. This is called ⬚. The Bible comes in two parts: the ⬚ ⬚ and the New ⬚. Altogether, there are 72 ⬚ in the Catholic Bible.

2. Read again the facts about the Bible. Try to put some of them into a 'Bible acrostic'.
Here's an example of how you could start.

Believed to be holy by Christians
I
B
L
E

3. Write each key word and explain in <u>one</u> sentence what it means. BIBLE, REVELATION, OLD TESTAMENT, NEW TESTAMENT.

4. The answer is '**the Bible**'. Can you write down five different questions: Example: What book is thought to have been studied and read by most people?

5. (a) Church Law states that the lectern should be fixed solidly, not moveable.

What does this symbolise about the Word of God?

(b) Some lecterns have an eagle carved on them.

What might this symbolise?

This is a Lectern.
The Word of God is read from here.

Extension

6. 'The Bible is one Book of many books, with one Author through many authors, and with one Word in many words.'

Can you explain the sentence above?

Glossary

Use the glossary to look up the following words: BIBLE, REVELATION, INSPIRATION, TESTAMENT, LECTERN.
Start your own glossary at the back of your book. Try to use your own words as much as possible.

An overview of the Bible

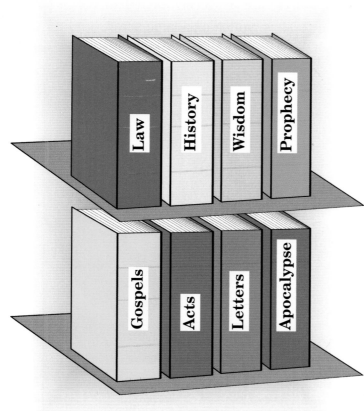

Old Testament

Law - the first five books of the Old Testament containing rules for living; for example: Exodus, Numbers.

History - the story of the Israelites and their kings; for example: the Book of Joshua, the Books of Kings.

Wisdom - poems, proverbs and other wise writings; for example: the Book of Psalms.

Prophecy - messengers sent by God to speak out God's message to Israel; for example: Isaiah, Micah.

New Testament

Gospels - the good news of Jesus' life, death and resurrection; for example: Luke's Gospel.

Acts of the Apostles - the story of the early Church.

Letters - letters written by apostles to different Christian communities; for example: St Paul's Letter to the Romans.

Apocalypse - describes the end of the world and the victory of Jesus *(told using mysterious symbols and images)*.

Activities

1. Using your knowledge and understanding of the Bible and its books, design either:

(a) a Bible bookmark. You should show on your bookmark the different types of writing in the Bible. You might also want to write a line from the Bible that's special to you.

(b) a suitable front cover for a Bible. Your cover should be an attractive design in words, pictures and symbols of the different kinds of books in the Bible.

Activities

2. Answer each of these questions with a full sentence.

(a) How many testaments are there in the Bible?
  (i) one.
  (ii) two.
  (iii) three.

(b) What is the first book of the Bible?
  (i) Matthew's Gospel.
  (ii) Genesis.
  (iii) Acts of the Apostles.

(c) What is the last book of the Bible?
  (i) Apocalypse.
  (ii) Deuteronomy.
  (iii) Mark's Gospel.

(d) Which books of the Bible do the Jewish people consider holy?
  (i) the four Gospels.
  (ii) the Old Testament books.
  (iii) the Letters of Saint Paul.

3. The **Qur'an** is the holy book for Muslims. The Qur'an is treated with great respect and care by Muslims. For example, the Qur'an is kept in a high place in a room to show how highly it is valued.

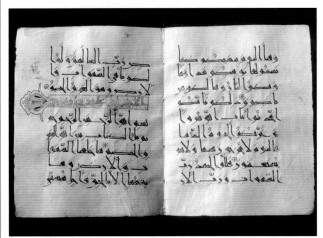

The Qur'an in decorative script.

The **Torah**, the first five books of the Hebrew Scriptures, are especially sacred to the Jews. The Torah is written on a large scroll.

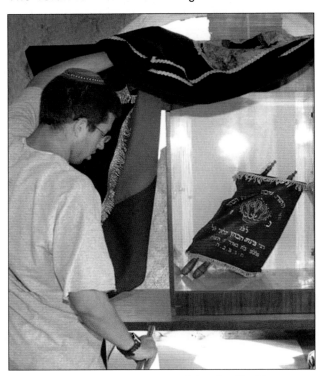

The Torah being prepared for the Shabbat Celebrations.

A Jewish reader in a synagogue will not touch the scroll. A small pointer is used instead.

Under a heading 'Treating the Bible with Respect', write down five simple rules to follow when handling or reading the Bible.

Follow up

WORKSHEETS
THE BOOKS OF THE BIBLE

TYPES OF WRITING IN THE OLD AND NEW TESTAMENTS

Glossary
PROPHECY, GOSPEL, MUSLIM, TORAH, HEBREW SCRIPTURES.

Looking up a Bible reference

The Bible contains thousands of words. Without help it's easy to get lost when looking for a particular book.

- When you look at the writing in a Bible you will see that the whole of the Bible is divided into *books*.

- The books are divided into *chapters*.

- The chapters are divided into *verses*.

- There are *big* numbers and *small* numbers in the paragraphs.

- The *big* numbers tell us the *chapter* whilst the *small* numbers tell us the *verse*.

- A Bible *reference* tells you where to look in a Bible for the lines you want.

- When you give a full Bible reference, it must contain the *book*, the *chapter* and the *verse*.

- An example is given below. The book is *Genesis*; the chapter is *chapter 1*; the verse is *verse 5*.

The book name is at the top of the page.

Genesis

1 ¹In the beginning God created the heavens and the earth. ²Now the earth was a formless void, there was darkness over the deep, and God's spirit hovered over the water. ³God said, 'Let there be light', and there was light. ⁴God saw that the light was good, and God divided light from darkness. ⁵God called light 'day', and darkness he called 'night'. Evening came and morning came: the first day.

Genesis 1:5

means the book of Genesis, chapter 1, verse 5.
⁵God called light 'day', and darkness he called 'night'. Evening came and morning came: the first day.

Glossary
BIBLE REFERENCE.

Activities

1. Here are some more Bible references, about places, things and people. The first pages of your Bible show how the Bible book names are shortened.

(a) Where did Noah's Ark come to rest after the flood? (reference Gen 8:4)

(b) What was the name of Moses' brother, the one who spoke for him? (reference Ex 4:14)

(c) What three things does God ask of his people? (reference Mic 6:8)

(d) At whose well did Jesus meet a woman drawing water? (reference Jn 4:5-6)

(e) On what was Jesus resting his head when a storm blew up? (reference Mk 4:38)

(f) What kind of tree did Zacchaeus climb to get a better view of Jesus? (reference Lk 19:4)

(g) What did Paul want his friends to remember? (reference Col 4:18)

Follow up
WORKSHEET
BIBLE SKILLS

How Christians use the Bible

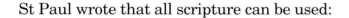

All scripture is inspired by God and can profitably be used for teaching, for refuting error, for guiding people's lives and teaching them to be holy. *(2 Tim 3:16)*

St Paul wrote that all scripture can be used:

- to teach people.
- to correct them when they go wrong.
- to guide people in living their lives.
- to show them the way to be holy.

Christians use the Bible *publicly* and *privately*. Publicly in shared worship - for example, in the Mass. Privately in meditation and prayer. It is important to prepare yourself to hear the Word of God.

Q. Whenever I hear the Bible being read aloud in Church, I find it difficult to concentrate. What should I do?

A. The Bible must be opened to be read; you must 'open yourself' to its message. You need to do more than hear; you need to *listen*. Read the story of Elijah in 1 Kings 19. He listened for the presence of God not in a mighty wind, nor in an earthquake, nor in a fire. It was the sound of a gentle breeze that told him of the presence of God.

Q. How can I read the Bible on my own? I try to understand passages from the Bible, but I get distracted easily. What should I do?

A. Sit still in a comfortable seat in a favourite corner. Read a small passage from, say, the Gospels. Read slowly. Close your eyes. Imagine yourself at the scene. Let the words sink deep into you. Hopefully, you'll begin to understand God's Word much more. Be patient and keep trying.

Activities

1. In what four ways did St Paul say that the Holy Scripture can be used?

2. The photograph below shows one of the first ever printed Bibles. Notice how beautiful the text and illustrations are.

(i) Choose some words from the Bible that are memorable and meaningful for you.

(ii) Write and decorate these words beautifully.

(iii) Write why these words are memorable and meaningful for you.

3. Organise a class Bible service. Your teacher will help you to do this.

Follow up
WORKSHEET
USING THE BIBLE

Extension

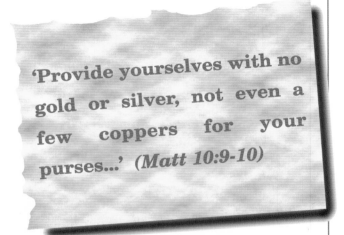

'Provide yourselves with no gold or silver, not even a few coppers for your purses...' *(Matt 10:9-10)*

4. These words are part of Jesus' advice to his disciples when he sent them out to preach. When St Francis of Assisi heard a priest read them out, they sunk deeply into him. He decided there and then to become a poor and wandering preacher.

Francis was with many others when he heard these Gospel words.

Why didn't some of them respond in the same way as he did?

Glossary
MEDITATION.

God's Self-Revelation

A number of young children were asked this question: 'What is God really like?' A selection of their answers is shown below.

"God makes everything grow"

"God can hear us"

"God is holy"

"God watches over us"

"God is the Father of Jesus"

"God is the biggest thing you can possibly imagine in the whole, wide world"

"God's always with you"

"God always loves you"

"God makes people happy"

Discuss

- What do you think of these answers - are they right or wrong?

- What would be your answer to the question: 'What is God really like?'

- Can words alone describe completely what God is really like?

The people of Israel probably asked the same question: *'What is God really like?'* God gave many answers throughout the Old Testament.

By listening to the books of Moses and the words of the prophets, the people of Israel grew in their knowledge of God, slowly but surely. At first, they might have seen God as a fierce protector, holy and just. Gradually, Israel would also come to see the gentleness and tenderness of God. So what is God really like? God gave a gradual answer. This is called *'God's self-revelation'*, or simply **'revelation'**.

God revealed himself to Moses through the burning bush.

Glossary
GOD'S SELF-REVELATION.

Activities

1. In **Genesis 15:1**, God said that he was Abraham's shield. Draw a large shield and use the following Bible references to create a shield. On this shield put words and pictures to show what God says about himself. Don't forget to include the reference next to each picture.

> Genesis 1:1
>
> **Hosea 11:10**
>
> Isaiah 49:16
>
> Psalms 23:1, 26:1, 27:1, 28:1
>
> Exodus 15:3, 15:18, 32:8

Extension

2. Think of the relationship between God and his People Israel as being like a journey. Here are four statements to describe this journey.

- God helped the People of Israel to know him better as the journey went on.

- The People of Israel knew exactly where God was leading them on this journey.

- The People of Israel did not know where God was leading them, but they had to trust that God would show them little by little.

- When God called Israel to be his People, the journey was over.

(i) Which statements do you agree with? Why?

(ii) Which statements do you disagree with? Why?

Follow up
WORKSHEET
GOD'S SELF-REVELATION IN THE OLD AND NEW TESTAMENTS

A Story

Once a Jesuit priest was leaving a small parish in South America. The people loved him. They all thanked him. A large, fierce-looking fellow came up to the priest. He told him, "Come with me". The large man pointed to his hut. The priest was unsure and a little afraid. He entered the hut and was told to sit down. The two men sat in silence. From the hut they looked out at the setting sun. The fellow said to the priest, "Señor, see how beautiful it is!" The two spent a few moments admiring the sunset. As the sun disappeared, the man said, "I do not know how to thank you for all you've done for us." He thought words weren't enough. Instead, he gave the priest a view of the beautiful setting sun.

Discuss
- Why didn't the man just say 'Thankyou' to the priest?
- Was his way of saying 'Thankyou' better than words?

Can words alone describe completely what God is really like? You were asked to discuss this on the previous page. Christians believe that it is impossible to sum up God in words alone. Instead, Christians believe that God gave one last Word. This last word was not a written word. It is Jesus.

What is God really like?

The answer is Jesus.

Jesus is Word of God in person. That is why John's Gospel says: **'The Word was made flesh and lived among us.'** *(John 1:14)*

The belief that God became man in Jesus is called the **'Incarnation'**.

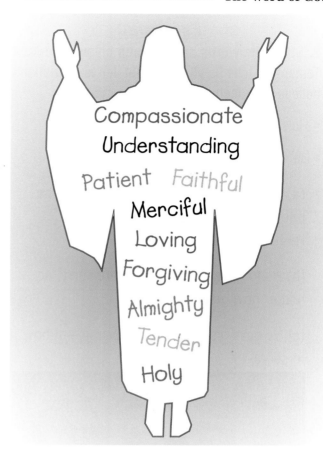

Compassionate
Understanding
Patient Faithful
Merciful
Loving
Forgiving
Almighty
Tender
Holy

Activities

1. Copy and complete the paragraph, using some of the words from the word bank.

From the N__ T_____ we learn a lot about Jesus. He was born into a poor, humble family. He was a c_____ until the age of thirty. He then began to preach the good news to the people of I_____. The good news was that God was with them. Jesus h_____ the sick, forgave s_____ and raised the dead to l____ again. He taught in p_____ about the goodness and love of God. He was betrayed and condemned to be c_____. He freely gave his life that others might live. He r____ again and told his d_____ to preach the good news of God's love to all p_____.

Word Bank

parables Testament Israel

people disciples love Christ

places shepherds hated crucified

healed carpenter rose

teaching new child

nice sinners pictures

life duties island

Glossary

INCARNATION.

Extension

2. Study the words and pictures below. The New Testament tells us all this about Jesus. Christians believe that Jesus is 'God-made-man'.

- He shows us what God is like.
- He shows us what God wishes us to be.

(a) Jesus preached the good news to the poor, and fed them in a lonely place. He healed the sick.

(b) He forgave sinners who were sorry, no matter how great their sin.

(c) He gave his followers an example of how to serve.

(d) He suffered for us.

(e) He died for us.

(f) He rose again. He promised a new life to all who believed in him.

3. Christians believe that Jesus is the answer to the question: 'What is God really like?'

Some helpful references

Matt 9:1-8, Matt 9:18-26, Matt 26:26-29,

Mark 6:30-44, Mark 6:53-56,

Luke 15:11-32, Luke 19:1-10, Luke 23: 39-43,

John 13: 3-5, John 15: 12-13.

What do the words and the actions of Jesus tell us about God?

(a) Write a paragraph to sum up what God is really like.

(b) Write a paragraph to sum up the type of person God is asking us to be.

Interpreting the Bible

Catholics believe that, without help, people can sometimes misunderstand the Bible.

Here are two common mistakes:

Mistake 1

"How can you trust the Bible - it says the world was made in 7 days?"

Reply

God speaks to people in a way they can understand. The People of Israel understood God's message through the stories of Creation written in Genesis.

Mistake 2

"The Bible, and only the Bible, is the Word of God'

Reply

Catholics believe that the Word of God is the Bible **and** Sacred Tradition. Sacred Tradition means the handing down of Church teaching from the Apostles onwards.

Let's have a closer look at these mistakes.

Mistake 1

"How can you trust the Bible - it says the world was made in 7 days?"

Reply

God speaks to people in a way they can understand. Otherwise what would be the point in speaking? Read the true story opposite of how a mother wishes to give an important message to her children.

Discuss

- What was the message the mother wished to get across?

- Did the girls understand the message?

- Why didn't the mother mention fast undercurrents and turbulence?

- Did the mother tell the truth? Explain your answer carefully?

- If you had been in the mother's position, how would *you* have explained the danger?

The mother used a **symbolic story** in order to get the truth across. The water pigs were a symbol of the hidden danger in the stream. The truth she wanted to say was this: *there is danger in the stream that you cannot see.* She had to tell this truth in a way the little girls would understand. In a similar way, God spoke to his people using language and symbols to help them understand deeper truths. God used a **symbolic story** to explain the truths about Creation.

The Message

In the late 1940s on a farm in Ireland there was a farming family - husband, wife and five daughters. The husband took suddenly ill and died, leaving the mother alone to cope with the farm and five young daughters. One of her great worries was the stream that ran by the farm. In summer, the stream was beautiful to look at. Yet at the same time it was dangerous. It had fast undercurrents that could easily sweep away a little girl.

She had to keep the little girls from danger and yet couldn't watch them every moment of the day. How could she get the message of danger across? She could have said that the stream had fast undercurrents, dangerous turbulence, swift hidden motions. But she didn't say this. How would the little girls have understood the message? Instead, she told all her daughters that the stream had dangerous water pigs hiding beneath the surface. The little girls were already afraid of the pigs on land, and so they always kept well away from the stream.

Activities

1. All the truths in the box below can be found in the two stories of Creation in the Book of Genesis. Working in pairs look up the references in the second box below and match them with the truths.

Truths Box

God made everything.

Everything God made is good.

God provides for all creatures.

God put human beings over the rest of Creation to help take care of it.

Reference Box

Gen 1:31,

Gen 2:15,

Gen 1:1,

Gen 1:29.

Extension

2. This story comes from Zambia, a country in southern Africa.

The Story

The hyena was greedy, as all hyenas are. This one was also hungry. It wandered along a bush track searching for food. It came to a fork in the track. Which way should it go? It raised its head and sniffed to the left. There was food there. It turned and sniffed to the right. There was food there, too. What should the hyena do? To go to the left might mean missing out on a better feast to the right. To go right might be to miss out on something delicious on the left. It tried to go in both directions, split itself in two and died.

Here are some opinions about this story.

'It isn't true- it's only a story.'

'It isn't true - hyenas can't split themselves in two.'

'It is true - greed does kill you.'

Which opinion do you agree with? Why?

Glossary
SYMBOLIC STORY.

Mistake 2

"The Bible - and only the Bible - is the Word of God."

Reply

Long before the Bible was collected together, the apostles like St Paul taught about Jesus. Because God's Spirit was with them, they preached the Word of God.

All of their teaching has been passed on from the apostles to those who come after them, the bishops. This is called **Sacred Tradition**. *It is like a flame passed from one generation to the next, like the Olympic flame is passed from one runner to the next.*

So the **Bible** *and* **Sacred Tradition** *are the* **Word of God**.

- Before Jesus ascended to heaven, he promised to send the Holy Spirit to his apostles.

- The Holy Spirit guided the apostles (the Church leaders) to pass on and explain more fully the truth about Jesus.

- The same Spirit who guided the apostles guides their successors, the bishops, to explain the truth about Christ and hand on this truth.

- The 'handing on' of the truth about Christ is called **Sacred Tradition**. The Bible is sometimes called **Sacred Scripture**.

- For Catholics, the Word of God means both Sacred Tradition and Sacred Scripture.

Activities

1. For each of the questions choose the correct option and write your answer in a full sentence.

(a) Sacred Scripture means
(i) the Bible.
(ii) an old way of writing.

(b) Sacred Tradition means
(i) the Bible.
(ii) teaching handed down from the apostles.

(c) Whom did Jesus promise to send his apostles?
(i) the Holy Spirit.
(ii) John the Baptist.

(d) The Bible was collected together in its final form
(i) when Jesus rose again.
(ii) many, many years after the resurrection.

(e) The successors of the apostles are
(i) bishops.
(ii) kings.

(f) Catholics believe the Word of God to be
(i) the Bible alone.
(ii) the Bible and Sacred Tradition.

Glossary

SACRED SCRIPTURE, SACRED TRADITION.

2 God's Call
What is Prayer?

There are some common ideas about what prayer is. Here are some ideas:

> Prayer is asking God for what you want.
>
> Prayer is needed when you are in trouble.
>
> Prayer is saying things to God.
>
> **People pray in Church.**

Some facts about Prayer

The ideas in the box above have some truth in them. Now, though, it's time to get a better idea of what prayer is. Prayer is not just what these ideas say it is. So what is prayer? Prayer is a reply, an answer, a response. Prayer is not so much making a call to God. It's more like answering a call from God.

In Islamic nations, you will hear the call of a muezzin from a mosque. It is a call to prayer.

Devotees raise their hands in prayer at the end of the World Muslim Congregation in Tongi, a town near the Bangladesh capital.

- Prayer is a response to God's call.

- Prayer is a conversation with God. We need time to listen as well as to speak.

- Prayer requires effort. Prayer is 'raising your heart and mind to God'.

- There are many ways of praying, with words, without words (meditation), with song - in fact, we can make everything we do into a prayer. We can pray *always* and in *all ways*.

- Prayer is essential. Friends keep in touch; if they didn't, the friendship would die. In the same way, your friendship with God needs prayer if it is to grow strong.

- Christians believe that God always answers prayers. Some people think that God is stone deaf. But even stone is not deaf to prayer. Look at how the stone of the statue has been altered by the millions of praying hands placed upon it. God is not like stone. God is attentive to our every cry.

The stone has been worn away on St James' statue at the Cathedral of Santiago de Compostela.

Activities

1. Write out the four ideas about prayer again from the previous page, but in each one include '**not just**' to give a better idea. For example: 'Prayer is **not just** asking God for what you want.'

2. Write out this paragraph (opposite) on prayer, choosing the right options as you go.

All prayer happens because **we call God to prayer/God calls us to prayer**. All prayer is **talking at/a conversation with** God. People need to **listen/speak as much as they can** during prayer. People pray **just/not just** in church or when they need God's help. There are **many/only a few** ways of praying. We **need/don't need** to pray if our friendship with God is to grow. Prayer requires **no effort/effort**. Prayer is a raising of our **hearts and minds/our voice** to God.

PRAYER QUESTIONNAIRE

3. Fill out the questionnaire:

1. How often do you pray?
(a) hardly ever ❏
(b) sometimes ❏
(c) twice a day ❏

2. When you say a prayer you've learnt, do you think about what you're saying?
(a) hardly ever ❏
(b) sometimes ❏
(c) as much as I can ❏

3. When you pray, do you include prayers in your own words?
(a) hardly ever ❏
(b) sometimes ❏
(c) quite a lot ❏

4. Someone says they're too busy to pray. What do you think?
(a) Shame ❏
(b) Are you sure? ❏
(c) Impossible ❏

5. Someone says that God hasn't heard their prayers. What do you think?
(a) Shame ❏
(b) Are you sure? ❏
(c) Impossible. ❏

6. St Paul says that we should pray at all times. What do you think?
(a) Impossible ❏
(b) Very difficult ❏
(c) I'd like to learn ❏

7. What is most important if you are to pray well?
(a) a big prayer book ❏
(b) a quiet room ❏
(c) trust and hope in God ❏

Every (a) scores 0 points.
Every (b) scores 3 points.
Every (c) scores 5 points.

Glossary
MUSLIM, MOSQUE, MEDITATION.

Follow up
WORKSHEET PRAYER QUESTIONNAIRE

Types of Prayer

There are perhaps four main types of prayer. These are explained in the boxes below. For each type an example from the Psalms is also given.

Asking: Petition & Intercession

When we ask God for help for ourselves (**petition**) or for someone else (**intercession**).

'I cry to you, Yahweh, my Rock! Do not be deaf to me...' *(Psalm 28:1)*

Sorrow

When we say sorry to God for something we have done and ask forgiveness.

'Have mercy on me, O God, in your goodness. In your great tenderness wipe away my faults...'
(Psalm 51:1)

Thanksgiving

When we thank God.

'I thank you, Yahweh, with all my heart, because you have heard what I said...' *(Psalm 138:1)*

Praise and Adoration

When we praise and adore God the Creator of all.

'Praise Yahweh, my soul! I mean to praise Yahweh all my life...'
(Psalm 146:1-2)

Activities

1. From the Gospel of Luke. Read **Luke 17:11-19.**

(i) What types of prayer do you see in this Gospel passage? List them.

(ii) Why is it that when we pray, it is often to **ask** rather than to **thank** God?

2. Copy this sentence and try to complete it:

'Some prayer is asking, thanking or saying sorry, but all prayer is…'.

3. Some people like to spend some minutes on their own in a church. They like to be silent in the presence of God.

Do you think that this is praying? Give reasons for your answer.

4. People make mistakes about prayer. Look at the *pictures A, B and C*, and explain the mistake being made. Set your answers out like this:

In Picture………, the person has made the mistake of……… The reason why this is a mistake is because………

Picture A: 'I'm too busy to pray…'

Picture B: 'In case you forget, God, I've made a list of my prayers…'

Picture C: 'Jimmy, it's your turn next…'

5. God always answers prayers of petition and intercession. Someone said that God may give four possible answers: *Yes, No, Wait* and *If.*

Can you explain them?

Example: 'YES' Your prayer has been heard and you will receive what you ask for because that would be good for you.

6. Some people light a candle when they make a prayer.

Why do you think they do this?

A boy lights a candle to make an offering in the chapel of Our Lady of Aparecida, Brazil.

7. Read the story below.

A Story

The weather forecaster promised that there'd be very heavy rain. People began to prepare. The rain came as promised and soon the streets were flooded.

The local council sent a truck round to evacuate people. Everyone in the flooded streets went except for one man. He stayed behind saying, "I trust in God. He will save me." The rain continued and the flood waters grew higher. The man went upstairs. The council sent a motorboat out to rescue him. He shouted from the bedroom window, "I trust in God. He will save me." The flood waters kept rising, and the man had to climb out through the window onto the roof. The council made one last bid to rescue him. They sent a helicopter and dangled down a rope ladder. "Get on!" they cried from the helicopter. "Don't worry", the man said, "God will rescue me." As the flood waters swamped the house, the man drowned. At the gates of heaven the man demanded to know why God had not answered his prayers. A voice said, "I sent you a truck, a motorboat and helicopter. What more did you want?"

What, in your opinion, is the main message in this story?

Glossary
PETITION, INTERCESSION, ADORATION.

Teach us to Pray

The disciples said to Jesus:
"Teach us to pray."
Jesus taught his disciples by:

- being a man of prayer.

- the teaching on prayer he gave.

- giving them a special prayer - the 'Our Father', or the Lord's Prayer.

What can we learn about prayer from what Jesus did and said? He made time for prayer, slipping away to a lonely place to be with his Father. He said how important it was to trust in God when you pray. At important or difficult moments in his life Jesus prayed for strength and guidance.

Jesus spent many hours with the twelve apostles, teaching them many things including how to pray.

Activities
(individually or in pairs)

1. If you look up the references you'll find seven lessons about prayer.

(i) Write down each lesson beside the reference that fits.

(ii) Write a small quote from the reference that sums up the lesson about prayer.

For example: Jesus made time and space for prayer. *(Mark 1:35)* '...long before dawn, he got up ...and went off to a lonely place and prayed there.'

Gospel References
Mark 1:35, Luke 11:9-10,
Matthew 6:7-8, Luke 6:12-13,
Luke 23:34, Luke 22:42,
Luke 18:13-14.

Lessons about Prayer

1. Jesus made time and space for prayer.

2. Jesus prayed when there were big decisions ahead.

3. Jesus prayed for strength.

4. Jesus prayed for others.

5. Jesus taught that you should be simple in your praying.

6. Jesus taught that you should be humble, not full of pride, when you pray.

7. Jesus taught that you should have faith, keep on praying and never give up.

Extension

2. Christians believe that Jesus is truly God as well as truly man. Why, then, did Jesus pray? Write five sentences. You must match the middle and end parts of each sentence.

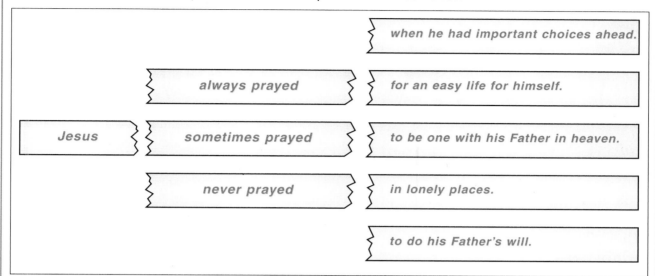

when he had important choices ahead.

always prayed

for an easy life for himself.

Jesus — sometimes prayed

to be one with his Father in heaven.

never prayed

in lonely places.

to do his Father's will.

Research

In the city of Jerusalem there is a part of the ancient Jewish temple called the '**Western**' or '**Wailing**' wall. Jews from all over come to pray there, placing prayer wishes between the stones. Pope John Paul II did the same during his visit in March 2000.

Find out about this place and explain in your own words why it is so sacred to Jewish people.

The Lord's Prayer

Jesus also gave his followers a prayer. This Prayer is the Lord's Prayer or 'Our Father'. This prayer is the main prayer of all Christians.

Our Father,
who art in heaven,
hallowed be thy name.
Thy kingdom come.
Thy will be done on earth, as it is in heaven.
Give us this day our daily bread,
and forgive us our trespasses,
as we forgive those who trespass against us,
and lead us not into temptation,
but deliver us from evil.
Amen.

Activities

1. (i) List the words in the Lord's Prayer that you do not use or know.

(ii) With your teacher's help write down what these words mean.

2. Read each part of the Lord's Prayer in the boxes opposite.
(i) Discuss with a partner what choice you'll make for the meaning of each part.

(ii) Write out the nine sentences, trying to chose the correct meaning for each one.

Follow up
WORKSHEET
MEANING WHAT WE PRAY

1. '**Our Father**' means - God belongs to us. - We belong to God.

2. '**Who art in heaven**' means - God is very close to us and yet greater than what we can imagine. - God's a long way away from us.

3. '**Hallowed be thy name**' means - We should make God's name holy. - God's name is holy, and we should remember this.

4. '**Thy Kingdom come**' means - Let God be King in some people's hearts. - Let God be King in all people's hearts.

5. '**Thy will be done on earth as it is in heaven**' means - Let what God wants always be done here. - Let what God wants sometimes be done here.

6. '**Give us this day our daily bread**' means - Give me now what I want. - Give us all today what we need.

7. '**And forgive us our trespasses, as we forgive those who trespass against us**' means - Forgive us our sins if, and only if, we are willing to forgive others. - Forgive us our sins, and we **might** forgive what others have done to us.

8. '**And lead us not into temptation, but deliver us from evil**' means - Give us the strength to fight bad thoughts when they come. - Don't ever let us be tempted to do wrong'.

9. '**Amen**' means - That the prayer is over, finished, complete. - I agree with this prayer and let it be so.

Annunciation and Visitation

Annunciation

Angels are pure spirits created by God. The word 'angel' is from a Greek word **'angelos'** which means **'messenger'**. Angels are God's messengers. Angels are mentioned in various parts of the Bible. They guide and protect people. Often, they deliver God's messages. Read the story of the Annunciation *(Luke 1:26-38)*, when the Angel Gabriel announced to Mary that she was to be the Mother of God's Son.

Mary gave a pure and simple "yes" when God called her to be the mother of his Son. Mary's yes was very special. It allowed the Saviour of the World, the Son of God, the Messiah to be born. The people of Israel had long believed that one day there would be a Messiah, a new king descended from King David. The Messiah would bring God's Kingdom to earth. Christians believe that Jesus is the Messiah.

Visitation

After the news that she is to be the mother of Jesus, Mary journeys south from Nazareth to see her cousin, Elizabeth. But the journey is not easy, perhaps about sixty miles through rough and dangerous trails. Elizabeth is filled with joy at the sight of Mary, her young cousin. Elizabeth and the child within her, John the Baptist, are filled with the joy of the Holy Spirit. Read the story of the Visitation, when Mary visited Elizabeth. *(Luke 1:39-45)*

Activities

1. Who am I?

(i) I was a great King in Israel; the Messiah was to be descended from me.

(ii) I was sent to prepare a way for Jesus; Elizabeth was my mother.

(iii) As a very young woman, I was visited by an angel who announced to me that I was chosen to be the mother of Jesus.

(iv) I said to Mary, "Of all women you are the most blessed."

(v) I was sent by God to announce to Mary that she was to be the mother of God's Son.

(vi) I was the husband of Elizabeth.

(vii) I was the husband of Mary.

2. Whenever someone asks you a favour, something you're not too sure of, you might not say yes. If you do say yes, it might really be a **"yes but..."** or a **"yes if..."**.

Mary answered God's call with what kind of "yes"? Pick from the box below and explain your choice.

"Yes.. ...but not now."

"...I agree to do whatever you want"

"...if you give me time."

"...if you pay me back."

"...if you do me a favour."

3. Re-read the story of the Annunciation and Visitation.

(i) Copy and complete these two lists of what the Angel Gabriel and Elizabeth say about Jesus and about Mary.

About Jesus
"He will be great"
....

About Mary
"She is highly favoured by God"
....

4. Use the two lists to write a paragraph in your own words on:

(i) What Catholics believe about Jesus.

(ii) What Catholics believe about Mary.

Glossary
ANGEL, ANNUNCIATION, VISITATION, MESSIAH.

Advent

Advent is a special time in the Church's year when Christians prepare for the coming of Jesus. Advent is a word that means 'coming'. The Season of Advent is a journey of four weeks leading up to Christmas. The Sundays of Advent are like the milestones in the Church's journey. You will see an Advent wreath in churches, with a candle to be lit on each of the four Sundays. This is a symbol of Jesus, the Light of the World, dawning on people who have lived in darkness.

John the Baptist, the son of Elizabeth, grew up to preach about the coming of the Lord. He told the people to repent and prepare the way for the Lord. He wanted everyone to be ready for Jesus. Today, Christians prepare for Jesus' coming by repentance and prayer. Repentance means turning away from sin, which can block the way of the Lord.

In Advent the priest will wear purple. Purple is a symbol of repentance and hope. There are *three* ways to think of Jesus coming to us, three aspects to Advent:

**A priest celebrates the Mass
wearing the purple vestments of Advent.**

- past - the infant Jesus coming into the world just over 2000 years ago.

- present - Jesus coming to us in our daily lives, especially in the disguise of the needy.

- future - Jesus coming again in glory at the end of time.

An Advent Wreath

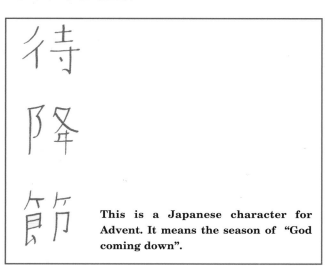

待降節

This is a Japanese character for Advent. It means the season of "God coming down".

Activities

1. Imagine that people sent Advent cards instead of Christmas cards.

Think of the meaning of Advent. Design an Advent card. Include an Advent message in it.

Make sure your Advent card would not be confused with a Christmas card. Some ideas are given, but you should try to think of your own too.

Images
Road to Bethlehem with four candles lighting the way.
Advent wreath.
John the Baptist preaching.

Messages
Wait for the Lord.
Prepare the way for the Lord.
O come, O come, Emmanuel.
We wait in joyful hope for the coming of our Saviour, Jesus Christ.

2. *'Get ready for Christmas!'*
Here's Tom's list of things to do for Christmas.

TOM'S CHRISTMAS
-to do LIST-
order turkey,
go Christmas shopping,
write and send cards,
wrap presents,
make mince pies,
order Christmas tree,
put up decorations.

What would a Christian say is missing from this list? Explain.

Extension

'Jesus is the reason for the season.'

3. Do you think it's easy to forget this notice (written on a Church board in December) in the weeks before Christmas? Explain your answer.

Research

The word **'maranatha'** is Aramaic. This is the language Jesus spoke. It was used in the prayer and worship of the early Church. Find out what it means.

The 'Lord's Prayer' in Aramaic

Glossary

ADVENT, REPENTANCE.

Nativity

Read the story of the Nativity, the Birth of Jesus. *(Lk 2:1-20)*

Christians believe that God became truly man in Jesus. This is called the **'Incarnation'**. How was God born into our world? God is awesome. Human life is humble. So when God becomes man, the awesome meets the humble. The story of the nativity has some awesome details and some humble details.

God does things differently to us. 'My ways are not your ways', says the Lord *(Isaiah 55:8)*. A new king is born surrounded by the riches of his kingdom - palaces, jewels, luxury. But Jesus' kingdom is not of this world. As the King of Heaven, he is born surrounded not by the riches of earth but by the riches of heaven - love, humility, peace and the voices of angels.

Discuss

- What awesome details are there in the story of Jesus' birth?

- What humble details are there in the story of Jesus' birth?
  (Use Mt 2:9-12, Lk 2:1-20)

"Thou shalt know him when he comes,
Not by any beat of drums,
Not the vantage of His airs,
Nor by anything He wears,
Neither by His crown, nor gown...
But His coming known shall be,
By the HOLY HARMONY,
His presence makes in thee."
(14th Century, Anonymous, England)

Activities in small groups

1. The most important person in the world is about to be born. What would you expect to happen before and as this person is being born? Use the list below to make up your answer.

- **Place of birth** - London, New York, Paris, Tokyo, Los Angeles?

- **First to get the news** - government, royalty, press?

- **Preparations** - clothes, maternity ward, nursery, toys?

- **Transporting mother to birth room** - limousine, police escort, helicopters?

- **Medical team** - top doctors, team of nurses, security guards?

- **Celebrations** - fireworks, parties, grand dinners?

2. Christians believe that Jesus is the most important person ever born. They believe he is both truly God and truly man. Use Luke 2:1-10 and the checklist in 1. above to describe the birth of Jesus.

3. Why was the birth of Jesus so different from the birth of an important person of the world?

4. The crib was first used by St Francis to show the poverty and humility of Jesus' birth. Read the following story about a crib by Frank O'Connor, an Irish writer.

Story

One Christmas, Santa Claus bought me a toy engine. I took it with me to the convent, and played with it while mother and the nuns discussed old times. But it was a young nun who brought us in to see the crib. When I saw the holy child in a manger, I was distressed because little as I had, he had nothing at all. For me it was fresh proof of the incompetence of Santa Claus. I asked the young nun politely if the holy child didn't like toys, and she replied, 'Oh, he does but his mother is too poor to afford them.' That settled it. My mother was poor too, but at Christmas she at least managed to buy me something - even if it was only a box of crayons. I distinctly remember getting into the crib and putting the engine between the holy child's outstretched arms.
I probably showed him how to wind it as well, because a small baby like that would not be clever enough to know. I remember too the tearful feeling of reckless generosity with which I left him there in the nightly darkness of the chapel, clutching my toy engine to his chest.
('An Only Child', by Frank O'Connor.)

(i) A toy engine is a very small gift. What made it so special?

(ii) What gift would Jesus want today from people at Christmas?

5. Look at various Christmas cards. Which one out of your selection gets across to you the meaning of Christmas? Explain your answer.

Follow up
WORKSHEETS
PRESENTATION OF THE CHILD JESUS
THE FINDING OF THE CHILD JESUS

Glossary
INCARNATION.

More about Mary

During the Visitation, after Elizabeth greeted Mary, Mary spoke out a poem called the Magnificat. It begins like this:

'My soul proclaims the greatness of the Lord and my spirit rejoices in God my saviour; because he has looked upon his lowly handmaid.
Yes, from this day forward all generations will call me blessed,
For the Almighty has done great things for me...' (Luke 1:46-49)

What are these 'great things'?

● God protected Mary from Original Sin.

Mary was chosen by God to be the mother of Jesus. Because of this, Catholics believe she was prepared in a special way. Since God the Son would take his human nature from her, her human nature had to be perfect. Therefore, God worked a miracle for Mary at the very beginning of her own life. He protected her from the damage of original sin. Unlike any other person, the conception - or start - of Mary's life was **immaculate**. This means 'spotless'. She was as perfect as Eve had been at the beginning. Catholics call Mary the **Immaculate Conception**.

● Mary is the Mother of God.

Christians call Mary the Mother of God. Jesus did not have a human father. The Holy Spirit began the baby growing inside Mary. Mary was the mother of that baby, and the baby was God-made-man. Therefore Mary was the mother of God. It does not mean that Mary is divine. She was just a human being; but her son Jesus is truly God and truly man.

Mary, a model of Faith

Christians call Mary their 'Model of Faith' because she gives them an example of how to trust God even when you don't know how things are going to work out. Mary is not God. She is a human being. She was only a teenager when Gabriel brought God's request to her. She shows us how to say 'Yes' to God and to trust God even when things seem strange and difficult.

A young boy prays to Mary at the 'Lady' chapel.

Activities

1. Write a sentence to answer the following questions.

(a) Mary's poem of praise to God is called...

(i) the Magnificat.
(ii) the Gloria.

(b) Catholics believe that God protected Mary from...

(i) all kinds of sorrow.
(ii) Original Sin.

(c)To call Mary the 'Immaculate Conception' is to believe that...

(i) she was spotless from the first moment of her life.
(ii) she committed only little sins.

(d) To call Mary the Mother of God is to believe that...

(i) she is God.
(ii) her son is God.

(e) To call Mary a Model of Faith is to believe that...

(i) she gives a great example of how to have faith in God no matter what.
(ii) her faith in God was never tested.

2. An icon is a beautiful image treasured by Christians, especially Eastern Christians.

(a) Trace the outline of the icon into your book.

(b) Colour the icon as follows:
(i) the mantle (outer cloak of Mary) in blue,
(ii) the tunic (inner garment of Mary) in red,

(c) Some believe that blue was used to signify being a mother, and red being a virgin. Others believe red signified Mary's earthly life and blue her sharing in Jesus' heavenly life. If this is so, what do the colours of Mary's clothes signify?

(d) Notice the star on Mary's veil. This reminds Christians of one of her titles: **'Star of the Sea'**. Why do you think she has this title?

(e) In all icons of Mary her eyes are large and her mouth is small. What do you think that these details could symbolise?

Glossary
MAGNIFICAT, DIVINE.

Hail Mary, Glory Be

After the 'Our Father', the 'Hail Mary' and the 'Glory Be' are the most widely known prayers among Catholic Christians.

Hail Mary

Hail Mary, full of grace,
the Lord is with thee.
Blessed art thou among women,
and blessed is the fruit of thy womb, Jesus.
Holy Mary, Mother of God,
pray for us sinners,
now, and at the hour of our death,
Amen.

The words of the 'Hail Mary' come from three sources.

- The first source is the Angel Gabriel's greeting to Mary: *"Hail Mary, full of grace! The Lord is with thee."* (see Luke 1:26-29) It reminds us that Mary was specially chosen by God to be the mother of Jesus.

- The second source is from Elizabeth's words to Mary, her cousin: *"Blessed art thou among women, and blessed is the fruit of thy womb".* (Luke 1:39-42) Mary is most blessed because of her simple obedience to God's call.

- The third source is from the Church, the People of God: *"Holy Mary, Mother of God, pray for us sinners now and at the hour of our death. Amen."* Because Mary is so close to her Son Jesus, she can intercede for us (pray to Jesus for us).

The Glory be

Glory be to the Father,
and to the Son,
and to the Holy Spirit,
as it was in the beginning,
is now and ever shall be,
world without end. Amen.

This is a simple prayer of praise to the Holy Trinity - Father, Son and Holy Spirit - three Persons, one God. Often, Catholics say the 'Our Father', 'Hail Mary' and 'Glory be' together.

The Rosary

The Rosary is a very old prayer. In this prayer the 'Our Father', the 'Hail Mary', and the 'Glory be' are said many times. Rosary beads are used to help a person pray the right number of 'Hail Mary' prayers. The beads stop us from worrying about numbers. Instead, we are asked to think about certain times in the life of Jesus and Mary. These are the *mysteries* of the Rosary.

There are five *Joyful* mysteries, five *Sorrowful* mysteries and five *Glorious* mysteries. Mary takes us around the 'rose garden' (Rosary) of the Good News of her Son's life, death and Resurrection.

Activities

1. Learn the '**Our Father**', the '**Hail Mary**' and the '**Glory Be**' by heart. (They can be found on pages 30 and 39)

2. Write a sentence, choosing the correct options.

(a) The first words of the Hail Mary are from...

(i) the angel Gabriel.
(ii) Elizabeth.

(b) The word 'thee' is an old fashioned word for...

(i) 'we'.
(ii) 'you'.

(c) 'The fruit of thy womb' means...

(i) Jesus.
(ii) John the Baptist.

(d) To 'intercede' means...

(i) to pray for yourself.
(ii) to pray for someone else.

(e) The 'Glory be' is a prayer of praise to...

(i) Mary.
(ii) the Holy Trinity.

(f) The word 'rosary' means

(i) rose garden.
(ii) necklace.

Extension

3. It's been said that in the Hail Mary we ask Mary's prayers for the two most important moments in our lives.

(a) What two moments are these?

(b) Why are they important?

Follow up
WORKSHEET **THE ROSARY**

Glossary
INTERCEDE, HOLY TRINITY, ROSARY.

3 The Sacraments
Signs and Symbols

Suppose you met someone from an unknown country. The stranger understands your language but is unable to answer. Instead, the stranger would make a sign - a gesture with his hands or body - to get across his meaning.

You ask this person some questions.

Your questions

- Are you from near or far?

- Do you come in peace?

- Are you happy to be here?

- Did you travel alone?

The answers he wants to give are:

His answers

- Far

- In peace

- Happy

- Alone

Discuss in small groups

- The gestures he would make that would get across each of the answers.

- You should find that different groups used similar gestures to answer the same question. Why is this?

Signs and symbols come naturally to us. We cannot do without them. **Signs** tell you something in a clear, understandable way. For example, road signs, weather signs and map signs.

Symbols are special signs. A symbol isn't to give you a quick instruction; it's to help you imagine something else. A red rose can be a symbol of romance; a dove often symbolises peace; a lighted candle can symbolise remembrance; a wedding ring is a symbol of love and faithfulness.

Discuss
- What other symbols can you name?

Activities

1. The word 'symbol' comes from a Greek word meaning 'to bring together'. Every symbol brings together something **visible** (that you can see) and something **invisible** (that you can't see but can imagine).

Copy and complete the table in your exercise book.

Symbol	
Visible – what you see	Invisible – What you imagine
Rose	Romantic Love
Wedding ring	
your example	
your example	

2. Read the story below about a lady's visit to an empty church.

A Story

The church is quite dark. Outside the traffic rushes by. Street lights, car lights and traffic lights play on the church windows. A woman pushes through the heavy church doors, dips a finger in the font and makes the Sign of the Cross. She looks towards the tabernacle and at the little sanctuary lamp flickering near it. She genuflects slowly. She walks up the aisle of the church and kneels in front of a statue of Our Lady at a side altar. After a few moments of prayer, she lights a little candle and then gets up. With one last glance at the crucifix hanging over the altar, she turns to leave.

(a) Lights are mentioned in this story.

(i) What lights are ordinary signs? Explain your answer.

(ii) What lights are symbolic signs? Explain your answer.

(b) There are some symbolic gestures (movements of the body) in this story.

(i) What symbolic gestures are there?

(ii) Can you explain what each of these gestures mean?

Glossary

SYMBOL, SYMBOLIC GESTURE, GENUFLECT, TABERNACLE.

We Need Signs

We need signs to communicate love

The most important message any person can communicate is a message of love. How does a mother show that she loves her tiny child? She cannot give a piece of love like a piece of bread. Her love is invisible. Shown below are some signs of love.

A present

A bunch of flowers

A message of love

A hug

Which sign will communicate love for the baby? Answer: the hug. Through the hug the baby would feel loved. Out of all these signs only one sign is a *living sign - a sign that is alive*. Love is alive and present in the sign of the mother's embrace. If the baby were not loved through living signs, she would not grow and develop as she should.

Read the article below about a professor's visit to an orphanage in eastern Europe.

The Way Today

24th July 2000

Hugs and Kisses are a must says American Professor

When the American Professor of Children's Health entered a room full of row upon row of wrapped up babies in the orphanage, she was struck by the silence. No babbling, no crying, not even a whimper. "The children were just lying there," said the Professor ... Research in this place has provided the first real evidence to show how the lack of physical affection - hugging, kissing - can cause harm to a baby's development.

To grow up properly a child must receive love through **'living signs'**. A baby is lost without love. Jesus said that everyone should be like a little child. Catholics believe that they receive Jesus' love through seven living signs called **Sacraments**. Each sacrament is like an embrace, because Jesus' love is really present through the sacrament.

Activities

1. Write the following sentences, saying whether they are true or false. Explain your answers.

Sentence	True or False
We can communicate without signs.	
A baby needs love to develop as he/she should.	
A sacrament is a living sign of the love of Jesus.	

2. Copy and complete the sentences below. Use the words in the word bank to help you. Some of the words will not need to be used.

Just as J[   ], during his life on earth, gave to the p[   ] he met, the l[   ], c[   ], f[   ] and m[   ] of God especially when they needed it most, so too in the C[   ] today the s[   ] are the s[   ] of the love and care of God brought into our lives by the r[   ] Jesus. The sacraments are s[   ] of Jesus' l[   ] in our l[   ]:

Word Bank

John   Jesus
love   people   love   signs
life   care   stages   celebration
forgiveness
cure   mercy   sacraments
money   sacrifices   royal
Church   songs   lives
risen   power   courage
ceremony   confirmation   like   signs

Extension

3. Read the story of a man who has suffered a huge stroke and cannot speak or move. His son Théophile and his daughter Céleste have come to visit him in hospital.

Story

Hunched in my wheelchair, I... watch my children as their mother pushes me down the hospital corridor. ...I will never tire of seeing them walk alongside me, just walking ...As he walks, Théophile dabs with a Kleenex at the thread of saliva escaping my closed lips. His movements are tender and fearful ...As soon as we slow down, Céleste cradles my head in her bare arms, covers my forehead with noisy kisses and says over and over, 'You're my dad, you're my dad,'... ('The Diving Bell and the Butterfly' by Jean-Dominique Bauby)

(a) What '**living signs**' of love do the children show their father?

(b) A few lines on in the book the father describes a feeling of terrible frustration inside him. Why do you think this is?

(c) One way of looking at the sacraments is as '**God's embraces**'. Why is this a helpful way to think about the sacraments?

Glossary
SACRAMENT.

Follow up
WORKSHEET **JESUS AND SACRAMENT**

The Story of Salvation

Catholics believe that people are not born in the state of grace and are distanced from God's life and friendship. This goes back to the *Fall*. In the Fall the first humans, Adam and Eve, fell from grace. This means they lost the joy and closeness of life with God because of their sin. They broke the close friendship they had enjoyed with God. Because of this all people since Adam and Eve are born in this state.

This is known as **'Original Sin'**. The transmission (passing on) of Original Sin is a mystery that we cannot fully understand. However, God didn't abandon us. He sent his son, Jesus, to bring us back to him. By his death and resurrection Jesus has opened the way back to the Father. The Church, the People of God, journeys to the Father. The sacraments of the Church are to give life and strength for this journey.

(Detail) of one of the Cherubim (one of God's Angels), casting out Adam and Eve from the Garden of Eden from a fresco (wall painting) by an artist called Masaccio.

The Sacraments

Marriage

Anointing of the sick

Holy Orders

Reconciliation

Eucharist

Confirmation

Baptism

The Journey of Life

Sometimes people think of life as a journey. It has a start and a destination. Some time after our journey begins, we reach a time when we can walk without help; then we can help others on their way.

Often through our journey we may fall or wander from the path. We need guidance and support from each other. We also need **'pathfinders'** to guide us on our way. We need food for our journey. We may find there are a number of different paths to the same destination; and we may walk a path with another close by. As we grow tired, perhaps near the end of our journey, we may need extra help and support.

Activities

1. Think of the Christian life as a journey. Copy and complete the sentences below.

(a) 'It has a start and a destination…'
The sacrament that marks the start of the Christian life is [   ].

(b) '…a time when we can walk without help'
The sacrament that marks the stage of Christian maturity is [   ].

(c) 'We need food for our journey.'
The sacrament in which a Christian receives Jesus as spiritual food is [   ].

(d) '…different paths to the same destination… another close by.'
The sacrament in which a Christian man and woman's love for each other is made holy in God's love is [   ].

(e) '…we also need 'pathfinders' to guide…'
The sacrament that makes a Christian man able to lead and guide God's people is [   ] [   ].

(f) '…we may fall or wander from the path.'
The sacrament that lifts up a Christian who has fallen is [   ].

(g) 'As we grow tired…'
The sacrament that heals and strengthens a Christian who is unwell or aged is [   ].

Extension

2. Here is the definition of sacrament from the **Catechism of the Catholic Church**. Write out this definition replacing the underlined words with your own.

'The sacraments are <u>efficacious</u> signs of <u>grace</u>, <u>instituted</u> by Christ and entrusted to the Church, by which <u>divine life</u> is <u>dispensed</u> to us. (para: 1331)'

<u>Meanings:</u> efficacious means 'effective', 'alive and active'; grace means 'God's help for our souls'; instituted means 'set up', 'founded' or 'put in place'; divine life means 'God's life' and dispensed means 'given out'.

Glossary

GRACE, DIVINE.

Initiation, Ministry and Healing

The sacraments of the Catholic Church may be put under three headings. Sacraments of *Initiation*, Sacraments of *Ministry*, and Sacraments of *Healing*.

Sacraments of Initiation

Initiation means 'bringing into membership of'. The sacraments of initiation draw a person fully into God's family, the Church.

- Through **Baptism** a person first becomes a Christian, receiving the life of God within them.

- Through **Confirmation** the Holy Spirit makes a Christian strong to be a witness for Christ in the world.

- In the **Eucharist** Jesus gives his pre-cious body and blood as spiritual food for the journey through life to heaven, our true home.

Sacraments of Ministry

These sacraments have to do with special ways in which Christians are called by God to serve in the Church. A minister is someone who serves God and others in a special way.

- In **Marriage** a man and a woman are made one by the grace of God. This grace will help them in their life together as husband and wife and, if God wills, as parents.

- In **Holy Orders** a man is given the authority (as deacon, priest or bishop) to act in Christ's place during worship and the sacraments and to lead God's people.

Sacraments of Healing

These sacraments have to do with: forgiveness, strength and healing.

- Through **Reconciliation** (Penance, Confession) Jesus forgives the sins of a person who is sorry and strengthens that person to follow him more closely.

- In the **Anointing of the Sick** a person who is ill receives inner healing so that they can be prepared to accept what God wishes and be at peace.

Activities
(Individually or in small groups)

1. Copy and fill in the table as shown below. Try to write (or draw) one or more symbol or gesture for each sacrament.

The word and picture bank (top of next page) shows some of the symbols and gestures used. You may think of others.

Sacrament	Symbol or gesture
Baptism	
Confirmation	
Eucharist	
Holy Orders	
Marriage	
Anointing the sick	
Reconciliation	

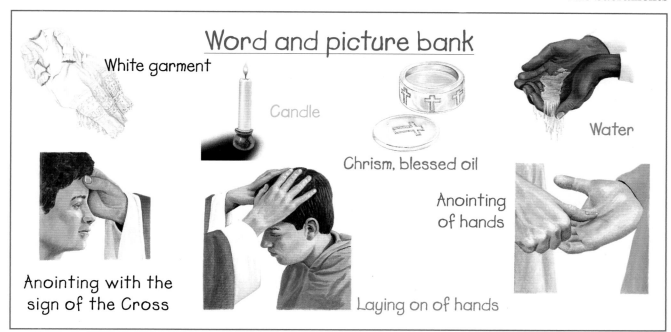

Word and picture bank

White garment

Candle

Chrism, blessed oil

Water

Anointing of hands

Anointing with the sign of the Cross

Laying on of hands

Activities

2. Read the story opposite. What sacraments does the old man talk about? Explain how you know.

3. Look at the picture below representing the seven sacraments.

(a) What does each letter stand for?

(b) Why do you think the 'E' is placed in the middle.

(c) Why is 'B' placed where it is?

(d) Whom does the dove represent?

(e) What do you think the big circle represents?

Story

Many years ago at a Native American settlement, a U.S. Government agent visited bringing such goods as waist-coats, shirts and tobacco. He saw an old Native American who he knew had become a Catholic. The agent joked with him, saying, "Your priest doesn't look after you; he doesn't seem to have brought you any presents, does he?" The priest could only visit very rarely.

The old man pointed to his chest and said, "Can you see into my soul?" The Government man said he could not. "Well, if you could you would see the beautiful white garment that God gave me when the Blackrobe baptised me. And every time he comes he washes it clean for me in the blood of Jesus Christ. And when he gives me commun-ion, he puts Jesus himself into my heart. Your tobacco soon goes off in smoke, and your shirts soon wear out, but the pres-ents that the Blackrobe brings will stay with me and take me to heaven."

Glossary

SACRAMENTS OF INITIATION, SACRAMENTS OF MINISTRY, SACRAMENTS OF HEALING.

Initiation

Activities

Read the following examples and try to notice what they have in common.

1. *For certain peoples, for example the Masai of East Africa, a boy becomes a man and a warrior only after passing through certain trials of courage and strength. In the past a Masai youth had to kill a lion as proof of his manhood. Usually, boys at the right age may be taken away from their village by a warrior. Under his guidance they have to learn to look after themselves in the wilderness for many weeks. Only after coming through these trials of strength and courage would a boy be initiated as a warrior.*

2. *Suppose a person wishes to become a citizen of the United States. This person would first have to qualify for citizenship. The person must pass the US Government's tests for qualification. Once the US Government is satisfied that a person qualifies to be a citizen then that person would have to make an official promise. This is the Pledge of Allegiance: 'I pledge allegiance to the flag of the United States of America and to the Republic for which it stands, one Nation under God, indivisible, with liberty and justice for all." The person can now become a citizen of the United States.*

1. After reading the two examples above, pick out things they both have in common. Copy and complete the table below into your exercise book.

EXAMPLE OF INITIATION	PREPARATION What must I do to prepare for the change to come?	CEREMONY/RITE What ceremony must I go through to mark the change?	IDENTITY How has the way I see myself changed?	RESPONSIBILITY What new changes must I make to the way I live my life?
Becoming a warrior				
Becoming a US citizen				
My own example				

Activities

2. Read this early description of how people became members of the Church. It was written to a Roman Emperor by a man called Justin, a Christian.

Dear Emperor

"I shall describe now the way in which persons are made new in Christ. They must believe Jesus to be the Son of God and Saviour and promise to live their lives in the way he taught. They must spend time fasting. They must pray and plead with God to forgive their sins, and we join them in fasting and prayer. Then we lead them to the water, and they are reborn. That is, they are bathed in the water in the name of God, the Father and the Lord of all things, of Jesus Christ our Saviour and of the Holy Spirit."

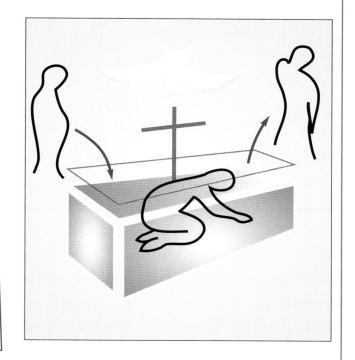

3. Read Justin's account again and copy and complete the table below into your exercise book.

EXAMPLE	PREPARATION	CEREMONY/RITE	IDENTITY	RESPONSIBILITY
BAPTISM	prayer, fasting learning about Jesus.			

Research

4. Research either:

(a) Baptist churches include very large baptismal fonts. Research the layout of a Baptist church.

Sketch, label and explain the key features inside a Baptist church.

or:

(b) In the rite described by Justin above, a person would have received all three Sacraments of Initiation. This still happens when a person is received into the **Eastern (Orthodox) Church**.

Research about initiation into the Eastern Church. Write up your findings **in your own words**.

Glossary
RITE.

Rite of Infant Baptism

The pictures show some of the main parts of the Rite of Baptism for baby Andrea. The Baptism may sometimes take place during the Mass. You can see a picture of the baptism itself on the next page. This is the time when Andrea becomes a Christian. This is why baptism is also given the name *christening*, because Andrea is marked with Christ's mark, the sign of the Cross.

- *A person is baptised only once.*

- *The baby's soul is cleansed from Original Sin and the baby restored to friendship with God.*

- *To show that baptism is the birth of a new Christian, a Christian name, Andrea, is given.*

- *Andrea's parents and Godparents promise to help Andrea to come to know, understand and live by the faith that is given her.*

---

1. Welcome

"You have asked to have your child baptised.

In doing so you are accepting the responsibility of training her to the practice of the faith..."

"Andrea, the Christian Community welcomes you with great joy. In its name I claim you for Christ our Saviour by the Sign of his Cross."

The priest welcomes Andrea, her parents and Godparents.

2. Bible reading and prayers

A passage from the Bible is read out to Andrea, her parents and Godparents.

3. Exorcism and Anointing with the Oil of Catechumens

"O God, you sent your Son to cast out the power of Satan; set this child free from Original Sin."

4. Baptismal Promises

"Do you reject sin, so as to live in the freedom of God's children?" "I do".

5. Baptism

The priest baptises Andrea.

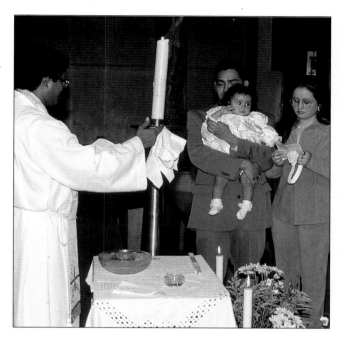

Andrea's white garment represents her new life in Christ.

Water is poured three times over the forehead while the priest says the words of Baptism:

"I baptise you in the Name of the Father and of the Son and of the Holy Spirit.'

6. Anointing with Chrism

7. White Garment and Baptismal Candle

The baptismal candle is lit from the Paschal candle.

"Receive the light of Christ. Parents and Godparents, this light is entrusted to you to be kept burning brightly".

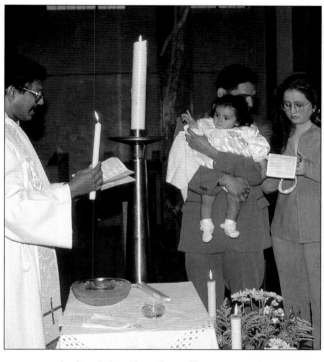

Andrea's baptismal candle represents Christ's light in her.

8. The Lord's Prayer and Final Blessing

Glossary
CATECHUMEN, CHRISM, PASCHAL CANDLE.

Follow up
WORKSHEET RITE OF BAPTISM

Symbols in Baptism

Among the symbols of Baptism are water, oil and light.

Water

Look at the following headlines. They are all about water. What different thoughts about water come to your mind as you read the headlines?

The Way Today
21st May 2000
Floods bring destruction in Bangladesh.

The Way Today
21st May 2000
CAFOD funds project to bring drinking water to fifteen villages.

The Way Today
21st May 2000
Are your work-tops clean? Studies show bacteria thrive on unwashed surfaces.

In Baptism, water symbolises:
- life - the new life of a Christian,
- cleansing - from original sin,
- death - to the old self you were before baptism.

Discuss
- Why in Baptism is water good to symbolise life, death and cleansing?

Oil

Throughout history oil has been used in different ways:
- When used on the body, certain oils can soothe and heal.
- Wrestlers use oil to make them difficult to grapple with.
- Some oils can bring softness and beauty to a face.
- The people of Israel used special oil to anoint those whom God had specially chosen (consecrated) to be a priest, prophet or king.

In Baptism:
- the Oil of Catechumens symbolises that the person has been healed and made strong.
- the Oil of Chrism symbolises that a Christian has received God's Spirit and is 'set apart' by God for his service.

Discuss
- In Baptism why is oil a good symbol of healing, strength, and being set apart?

Light
- We need light to see clearly. Without light we could not find our way.
- The light of a candle helps others to see.
- The light of a candle is gentle and warm.

Discuss
- Why do you think that light is such an important symbol in Baptism?

The picture below shows Christ, the Light of the World, standing at a door. When the artist had finished the picture, a friend told him that he'd forgotten to paint a handle on the door. The artist said that the handle was on the inside of the door. People must open the door to let Christ's light in.

Some thoughts about Baptism

> *"But Andrea looks no different after being baptised. Baptism hasn't done anything to her."*

Answer: If you plant a seed in soil and then cover it over, the soil looks no different to before. But given care, warmth and water, you will soon see the difference. In the same way, the *'seed of faith'* planted in Andrea will, with care, grow and blossom into a fully Christian life.

> *"Many people have their children baptised without thinking about it. It's just a ceremony that's over and done with."*

Answer: Baptism is not over when the rite is over. Andrea has a new life as a Christian. Her parents and godparents have promised to help her grow in knowledge and understanding of her faith.

> *"But Andrea is just a baby. How does she know what is going on? Shouldn't she be allowed to choose if she wants to be baptised?"*

Answer: Parents have the right to make good choices for their children. For example, they will choose Andrea's food, clothes and her first school. They make all those choices that Andrea cannot make yet. In the same way, they choose to have her baptised and to bring her up as a Christian.

> *"So being a Christian has got nothing to do with Andrea; it's to do with her parents and godparents?"*

Answer: Andrea's parents and godparents are very important in helping Andrea to understand her faith. As Andrea grows older, she will become more and more responsible for *'keeping the light of Christ burning brightly'*. She received a new life in Baptism, and so she must learn to live a new lifestyle. The new lifestyle Jesus wants is for Christians to love God, and their neighbour as themselves.

> *"Is the white garment that Andrea received a symbol to show she is always clean in God's eyes?"*

Answer: Through Baptism Andrea's soul is washed clean. The white garment is a symbol of being covered with Christ's purity. However, a white garment is easily made dirty. Stains show up clearly. So Andrea will always need God's help (grace) to remain clean in God's eyes.

Activities

1. Design either:

(a) an invitation card or

(b) a memento card for Andrea's Baptism.

- Include in your design the symbols of Baptism.
- Make up any details (for example: date, time, church, priest) for your card.
- Include on your card a short message which sums up the meaning of Baptism.

2. Write **one** sentence to answer each question.

(a) When does a person become a Christian?
   (i) when they are baptised.
   (ii) when they are aged 12.
   (iii) when they first pray to God.

(b) The anointing with what has the symbolism of strength and healing?
   (i) oil of Catechumens. (ii) oil of Chrism.
   (iii) pure olive oil.

(c) Where on the body is the infant given this first anointing?
   (i) forehead. (ii) top of the head. (iii) chest.

(d) From what candle is the child's baptismal candle lit?
   (i) one of the altar candles.
   (ii) the candle that lights the sanctuary.
   (iii) the Paschal Candle.

(e) What is signified by the white garment?
   (i) warmth and strength.
   (ii) being 'clothed with Christ'.
   (iii) protection of parents.

3. (In pairs) Imagine you are interviewing those present at Andrea's Baptism. Some questions to ask are shown above (next column). Use these questions to write a script with the answers you imagine would be given. You may wish to include one or two questions of your own.

Who is being asked	Questions
Parents	Why do you want Andrea to be baptised?
	Why did you choose to name your baby Andrea?
	How are you going to help Andrea grow in the faith?
God-parents	What duties do you have as the Godparents of Andrea?
Priest	Do you only baptise babies?
	You anointed Andrea on the forehead. What does that mean?

Extension

4. Read this letter from a newspaper.

Dear Virginia

My best friend has asked me to be god-mother to her first baby. She is religious, but I don't believe in God and am therefore unsure whether to accept. My husband says the promises mean very little and I should simply accept the invitation. My friend says it doesn't matter to her. But even though I don't believe in God, I still feel that to utter promises I don't mean would be wrong. Am I being silly?

Yours, Joanna

From your knowledge of the Roman Catholic rite of Baptism, write a thoughtful reply to this letter.

Research

5. The **Paschal Candle** is used to light the Baptismal candle. The Paschal Candle is full of symbolism. Research about the Paschal Candle. Draw, label and explain the symbolism of the Paschal Candle.

Glossary
CONSECRATE.

4 Sacraments of Healing

Genesis and the Problem of Evil

From where does evil come? Why is there so much trouble and suffering around us? People have always asked themselves these questions. The ancient people of Israel thought about these questions too. God answered some of their questions through the great stories in the Book of Genesis.

From where does evil come?

The first people disobeyed God. They wanted their way instead of God's way. They blamed each other for their sin.

What happened then?

They were sent away from God's presence. They had fallen away from God's friendship.

Does that make a difference to me?

When Adam and Eve fell away from God, all humans have fallen with them.

In what way does Adam's sin change us?

Human beings have inherited a deep fault. We find it harder to love God and to hate evil as we should. This is called Original Sin.

What happened after Adam and Eve left Paradise?

Well, one son murdered his brother. Then, wrongdoing spread like a disease. In their pride, people tried to create a world without God. Trying to live without God brings disaster. Then God sent the flood.

So the People of Israel knew:

- that evil in the world is because of bad choices made by humans.

- that sin leads to more sin.

- that sin brings destruction into the world.

- that God wanted to call human beings back to himself.

Activities

1. (a) Write a letter to God about what's wrong with the world. The start and the end are done for you.

Fill in the middle of the letter to God. Include things that upset you and seem unfair.

> Dear God,
> Why do You allow all the hatred and suffering to go on in the world? You could do something about it. You have the power...
>
> ...why are things like this?
>
> Yours faithfully...

(b) Imagine the 'reply' from God.

> *My child, forgive Me.*
> *Forgive Me for planting in every human the free will to choose. To choose My way or another, selfish way. Forgive Me for blessing you with talents to use for the healing of My world. You see, I have no hands on earth but yours. I help with your hands, comfort with your voice, spread joy with your smile. Forgive Me for asking you to love one another as I love each and every one of you, even when you leave Me. And then when you turn back to Me and admit the wrong you have done, forgive Me please, for forgiving you.*

Use this 'reply from God' to help you to write an explanation of suffering. Start with...

> **"There is evil and suffering in the world because..."**

Research

2. Cut out from newspapers and magazines words and stories about bad things happening. Make a collage of these. Give your collage a title - for example, '**Our Broken World**'.

Earthquakes in Turkey.

Floods in Mozambique.

Famines in Ethiopia.

True Freedom

One day, **False Freedom** met **True Freedom**. **False Freedom** said, *'Look at me; I serve no one, I obey no one. I am free to do whatever I want. Walk with me."* **True Freedom** agreed to walk with **False Freedom**. As they were walking they met **Rules**.

False Freedom said, *"What do you want? Get out of my way."*

Rules said, *"I don't mean any harm."*

False Freedom shouted back, *"Liar! You want everyone to follow you. Well, I'm not going to."*

Rules tried to defend himself: *"People only follow me because they need to."*

True Freedom said to **Rules**, *"It's all right, Rules, you can walk on my side."* They continued to walk, but **False Freedom** kept looking over angrily at **Rules**. Soon, they met a friend of **Rules** called **Responsibility**.

False Freedom screamed out, *"Don't come near me, Responsibility! You're always trying to make people face the consequences of their choices."*

"What's so bad about that?" asked **True Freedom**.

"Don't you get it?" said **False Freedom**. *"If I had to worry about the consequences of my actions I wouldn't be free to do whatever I want."* Whilst they were discussing, another person walked amongst them. *"What's your name, stranger?"* **False Freedom** asked.

"Some people call me Friendship, others call me Community," answered the stranger.
"Well," said **False Freedom**, *"come and walk with me because this lot are driving me nuts. Have you met them - Rules, Responsibility and True Freedom?"*

Community replied, *"Of course, they're all old friends of mine. We've been walking together for years."*

"That's funny," said **False Freedom**, *"I've never seen you before. Anyway, come my way, we'll have a great time. We'll serve no one, obey no one; we'll be free to do whatever we want."*

Community said, *"I'm sorry, but I can't possibly walk with you. The kind of life you lead would destroy me in a day."* So **False Freedom** sulked away on his own.

Discuss
- How would False Freedom describe himself?
- How would True Freedom describe himself?
- How would False Freedom destroy Community?

Freedom to choose

God loved us enough to give us freedom. God does not force us to do his Will. We are each free when it comes to choosing God's way or not. We can make good choices or bad choices. If I were not free no one could blame me for what I did; I could not be held responsible for my actions.

Christian Freedom

The Christian idea of freedom is not freedom to do what you want no matter what others feel. Christian freedom is freedom to serve God and others. This is true freedom. Jesus gave us a great example in his life on earth. He was obedient to the Will of the Father, not because he was forced to, but because he wanted to be obedient.

Activities

1. Copy and complete the sentences below.

> A time when I feel really free is when
> _____.
> Things that seem to block my freedom are _____.
> Things that seem to give me freedom are _____.
> My symbol for freedom would be _____.
> My definition of freedom is _____.
> If everyone had this freedom the world would be _____.

Extension

2. Read the story of Franz Jägerstätter.

Franz Jägerstätter was born in 1907 in a little village in Austria. He was quite a rowdy young man and didn't care too much for the Church, although he had been baptised a Catholic. When he married he calmed down and became more serious about his faith.

Meanwhile Hitler was calling up all young men from Germany and Austria to serve in his army and fight for Nazi Rule. Franz received an order to join the army. He refused to join because he believed Hitler's ideas and plans were evil. Twice more Franz was given orders to join the army. He still refused, believing in his heart that God did not wish him to be part of the Nazi war machine. Franz was now a father of three little girls; his friends and neighbours told him to join the army. They all knew that Franz would be imprisoned and executed if he continued to refuse. 'Think of your wife and family', was the constant message. Franz loved his family dearly, and yet he knew that to serve in Hitler's army would be to go against his conscience.

Franz Jägerstätter was imprisoned and executed for refusing to be a soldier for Hitler.

(a) Franz had a very hard choice to make. What things made his choice so hard?

(b) Some might say that Franz did a foolish thing in refusing Hitler - his wife was made a widow and his children lost their father. What would you say against this view?

Follow up
WORKSHEETS
WHAT IS MY CONSCIENCE?

Freedom and Responsibility

Can you be Trusted with Freedom?

Copy and complete this questionnaire into your exercise book. There's a code found by choosing the best answers. Can you work out the code?

FREEDOM AND RESPONSIBILITY QUESTIONNAIRE

1. A friend tries to get you to make a promise you don't want to make. Do you...

(s) say that you'll try to keep it? ☐
(t) say no and explain why? ☐
(v) promise anyway but don't keep it? ☐

2. You promise your Mum you'll be back from a friend's house at a certain time. Do you...

(r) keep your promise? ☐
(s) phone and ask for more time? ☐
(t) come back late and creep in? ☐

3. Your teacher tells you to stop talking. Do you...

(s) think - he's picking on me? ☐
(t) talk ever so quietly? ☐
(u) stop talking? ☐

4. You borrow something from a friend and promise to let her have it back. Do you...

(r) return it late? ☐
(s) return it promptly in good condition? ☐
(t) completely forget until reminded? ☐

5. You are working with a friend on a large project. Do you...

(t) do your fair share? ☐
(u) wait for your friend to tell you what to do? ☐
(v) let your friend do as much of the work as possible? ☐

6. Someone in your class is told off for something you did. Do you...

(k) think yourself lucky? ☐
(l) keep quiet but apologise to the person later? ☐
(m) own up and take the blame? ☐

7. Your friend is being badly bullied but he tells you to forget about it. Do you...

(d) try to forget about it? ☐
(e) tell him firmly he must tell a teacher otherwise you will? ☐
(f) stop being his friend in case you are bullied too? ☐

8. Now write a paragraph to answer the question: 'Can I be trusted?'

Activities

1. After doing the questionnaire, explain:

(a) those areas in which you can be trusted.

(b) those areas in which you need to become more trustworthy.

How would people treat you if you could not be trusted at all?

2. 'Suspect X then took a plate of spaghetti and threw it all over the waiter'

Explain how much to blame Suspect X would be if he or she was:

(a) an eight month old baby?

(b) a seven year old child?

(c) an adult?

3. (a) Read the article from a newspaper below. It is about something that really happened.

The Way Today

21st May 2000

100 mph Drink Driver Kills Young Woman

A father found his daughter dead after a drunken motorist crashed into her car at 100 mph.

The motorist responsible had already been charged with a previous drink-driving offence. He had been drinking for six hours in a public house when he bet a friend that he could set a record for driving to the junction of the motorway in his new car.

While trying to overtake another driver on the inside, he lost control of his car and crashed into the young woman's car......

'I didn't mean to hurt anybody. I wouldn't hurt a fly.'

(b) Suppose the drunken motorist had said this (see small box) in Court, would you believe him? Explain why or why not, using the words **'freedom'** and **'responsibility'** in your answer.

Glossary
TRUST, RESPONSIBILITY, CONSCIENCE, ORIGINAL SIN.

Do we need Rules?

(Sarah is on detention and has to report to Mrs Beresford, the deputy head.)

Miss, I'm here.

Well, come in, Sarah. Why have you been sent here?

For talking back, Miss.

Why did you do that, Sarah? You know the rules of this school.

I know, Miss. But I'm sick of rules, Miss. Everywhere you go - rules, rules.

You think we'd be better off without these rules?

Yes, Miss.

Sit down over there and get your books out.

Here, Miss?

Yes. Oh, by the way, Mr Elias said he'd also confiscated some sweets from you that I'm supposed to give back before you go home. The trouble is, I've eaten them.

Miss!

Delicious they were too - I love chocolate bonbons.

But Miss, that's stealing. I'm going to get my mum to come in.

Stealing - that's just a silly rule. We don't like rules do we? And as for your mother - I don't think I've ever met anyone so foolish. She can't even bring up her kids properly.

Don't speak about my mum like that!

Why not? Don't tell me you respect her?

Of course I respect her. Everyone should respect their parents.

That sounds like another rule. Anyway, I've already phoned your parents to invite them in to explain why their daughter has been sent out of class to me three times already this term.

But this is the first time this term. Miss, that's not fair!

I know, Sarah, but it's easier to get you suspended if I say three times rather than once.

Miss, that is so out of order. You're just lying to get me done big time.

Sarah, you can hardly expect me to obey a silly little rule about lying.

Activities

1. (a) Three rules mentioned are from the Ten Commandments. Write down these three rules.

(b) What is Mrs Beresford trying to get Sarah to understand?

2. Imagine one very simple, ordinary activity - for example, walking in the park, a bus ride, going shopping. Now imagine that all rules and laws have just been cancelled.

Describe how your '**ordinary activity**' is affected by the cancellation of laws.

Extension

3. Imagine you had to give a short talk to a class on '**Why we need rules**'. How would you use the story below as part of your talk?

The wood duck nests in the hollow of a tree about 40 feet off the ground. The ducklings can then hatch out safely. The wood duck then flies to the bottom of the tree and quacks at her ducklings. One by one they tumble the great distance, bounce off the earth and stand up unharmed. Once they're all down she takes them to the lake where they can feed and swim safely. If a duckling doesn't jump from the nest, it remains there and dies. The mother duck does not return to check whether her nest is empty.

What is Sin?

Imagine someone who loves you completely, who knows you better than you know yourself, who is tender, who thinks of your needs before you realise them yourself.

> It was you who created my inmost self, and put me together in the womb; and for all these mysteries I thank you: for the wonder of myself, for the wonder of your works.
> *(Psalm 139:13-14)*

Every sin is a rejection of this tender love of God.

What is sin?

Here are some explanations for what sin is:

- **being less than you were made to be.**
  Sin makes me less than the person God made me to be.

- **disobeying your conscience.**
  God has 'written his law' in our minds. To disobey your conscience is to sin.

- **breaking God's commandments.**
  The law 'written in our minds' is reflected in the Ten Commandments given by God through Moses. Following the Ten Commandments leads to life, so a person must *not* break them.

- **failing to love.**
  God is love. The greatest commandment is to love God and others. Sin is saying *no* to love.

- **an offence against God**.
  Most of all, sin offends God. For example, when we hurt our neighbour, we are hurting a child of God. God is offended when his children hurt each other.

The Effect of Sin

Whenever I sin, I separate myself from God and from others. Friendships are shattered, trust is broken, fear is born, enemies are made.

Activities

1. The picture above is taken from a story in **Genesis, chapter 3**. Tell the story in your words.

2. Jealousy and anger can break up a friendship in a family or in school. Show how 'step by step'.

"We used to be good friends"

"Now we don't speak to each other at all."

But then...

3. (a) The word '**SIN**' has '**I**' at the centre. What truth does this get across?

(b) Turn **EVIL** around and you get **LIVE**. What truth does this get across?

Jesus Seeking the Lost

God 'went out of his way' to call sinners back to him. He sent his only Son among us to save us. Jesus, true God and true man, met many people who needed forgiveness and healing. He refused no-one. He gave to all who wanted his help. The New Testament has many accounts of how a sinner decided to make a fresh start after meeting Jesus. Here are a few of these meetings told from the view of the sinner.

Before

Hello, my name's Thomas. I met Jesus a long time ago. For many years of my life I was paralysed and a beggar. I thought I was being punished for my sins and the sins of my ancestors. One day, just out of the blue, my relatives carried me on a stretcher to where Jesus was preaching. They couldn't get in the door, so they ripped open the straw roof and lowered me down.

After

...The crowds watched silently. Jesus looked down on me with such a beautiful warm look. He said, "Don't be afraid. Your sins are forgiven." I'll never forget it. I knew then in my heart that I was completely forgiven. Then because others were muttering about this, Jesus proved his power to forgive sins by healing me of my paralysis. He told me to take my stretcher off home. I did. I walked at first, then I danced for joy. An unforgettable day.

Before

Hello, I'm Paul or Saul - whatever's easier. Before I met Jesus I was a very strict Jew called a Pharisee. I believed that the followers of Jesus were traitors. I thought they were trying to twist the true Jewish faith. I knew Jesus had been crucified, but his followers were going around saying he'd risen from the dead. I was determined to stop them and so I went around trying to hunt them down, arrest them and imprison them.

After

One day I was travelling to a city called Damascus in Syria. I was hunting Jesus' followers. Suddenly a bright light shone from heaven. I was dazzled and fell to the ground. It scared me, I can tell you. A voice, Jesus' voice, asked, "Saul, why are you trying to hurt me?" I couldn't see or eat anything after that. Three days passed. A follower of Jesus called Ananias healed me in the name of Jesus. I became a follower of Jesus myself. In time, I preached about Jesus in many cities and towns. Now, I'm in prison because of this. But in my mind I'm happy and at peace.

Activities

1. Paul believed that it was Jesus' voice that he heard when he fell from his horse.

(a) In what way was he hurting Jesus?

(b) What message does Paul's story have for us today?

(c) Can you explain why Paul says he is happy and at peace?

Activities

2. Read Zacchaeus' story **before** and **after** he met Jesus.

(a) Read **Lk 19:1-10** and use the information below.

Before Zacchaeus met Jesus he was a tax collector. Others hated him because he collected taxes which were used to keep the Roman soldiers in the country. He would often cheat people by collecting more than he should. He had become very rich and was made chief tax collector in his area.

(b) What was Zacchaeus like before he met Jesus?

(c) What was he like after he met Jesus?

3. Read the story of **Onesimus** and **Philemon**. You will find it in the New Testament Letter of Paul to Philemon.

The Way Then

AD 61

Owner asked to forgive runaway slave.

(a) Onesimus was a runaway slave - a serious offence in those times. How did Paul get to know him?

(b) How did Onesimus change?

(c) What did Paul ask of Philemon?

Follow up
WORKSHEET **THE MERCY OF GOD**

Glossary
SIN, TEN COMMANDMENTS, FORGIVENESS, CONVERSION.

Forgive us our Trespasses

All sin is washed away in Baptism. However, because the white robe Christians receive at Baptism is all too easy to make dirty, Jesus gave his Church the **Sacrament of Reconciliation (Confession, Penance)**. In the Sacrament of Reconciliation, God welcomes back the sinner like the father welcomed back his lost son (in the parable). The forgiveness given is the same forgiveness the paralysed man or Zacchaeus received.

The Sacrament of Reconciliation involves *contrition*, *confession*, *penance* and *absolution*.

- **Contrition means being truly sorry in your heart for your sins.**
- **Confession means speaking out or confessing your sins.**
- **Penance means trying to repair the damage of your sins.**
- **Absolution means being completely freed from your sins.**

Rite for Individual Confession

1. Examination of Conscience

Before going to confession a person must examine their conscience. They should 'look deeply into themselves' to see the actions and attitudes that are wrong.

2. Confession of sins

A person confesses their sins:
'Bless me, father, for I have sinned. It is one month since my last confession...'

People confess their sins at an outdoor reconciliation service.

3. Advice and Penance

After listening to the person as they confess their sins, the priest offers advice and a penance so that the person can try to make up for the damage done by their wrongdoing.

The priest offers advice and a penance.

4. Act of Contrition

The person expresses their sorrow:
'O my God, because you are so good, I am very sorry that I have sinned against you, and by your grace I will not sin again.'

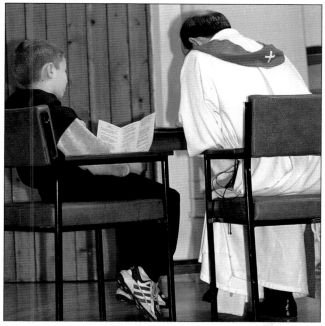

The young boy expresses his regret and sorrow to God.

5. Absolution

The priest stretches out his hand and says the Prayer of Absolution. This prayer ends:
'I absolve you from your sins in the name of the Father and of the Son and of the Holy Spirit.'
The forgiveness of Jesus comes to the person through the priest.

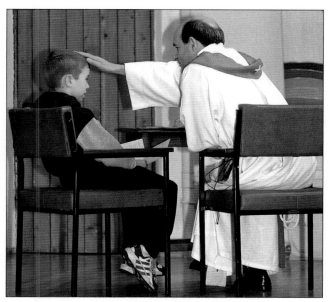

The priest gives Absolution.

Note the following:

1. In examining their conscience, a person is not just remembering a list of sins. They're also trying to uncover sinful attitudes *(like jealousy)* which lead to sinful acts.

2. In confessing to the priest, a person is confessing their sins to Jesus. The priest has a duty *never* to mention sins he has heard during confessions.

3. If a person is truly sorry for their sins, they'll try to repair the harm done by accepting a penance. This penance may be in the form of a prayer or an act of charity.

4. Another way of showing sorrow for what a person has done wrong is to make a strong wish not to do wrong again. In other words, to have a *firm purpose of amendment*.

5. Being forgiven is not the same as being 'let off'. Being tempted to commit sin is not the same as committing sin. Feeling bad after sinning *(remorse)* is not the same as being sorry *(repentance)*.

Activities

1. Copy and complete the table below.

Word	Meaning	Stage in the rite of the Sacrament of Reconciliation that matches this	Quote from Prodigal Son that matches this (see Lk 15:11-32)
Contrition	being sorry in your heart for your sins.	all the stages, especially Examination of Conscience.	At last he came to his senses... I will get up and go to my father.
Confession			
Penance			
Absolution			

2. Look back to the Act of Contrition said during the Sacrament of Reconciliation.
(a) There are three kinds of 'sorry':

> sorry because I've been caught;
> sorry because I'll be punished;
> sorry because I've hurt you.

Which kind of 'sorry' is in the Act of Contrition? Explain your choice.

(b) Make up your own Act of Contrition.

3. Write eight sentences using the beginnings and endings shown below.

It is impossible...   It is possible...
...for you to sin by complete accident.
...for you to commit a sin too great for God to forgive.
...for you to be forgiven if you won't forgive others.
...for you to commit a sin in your thoughts.
...for you to try to repair the damage of your sins.
...for you to be forgiven by God if you're not sorry.
...for you to commit a sin by not doing something.
...for you to go through life without being tempted to do wrong.

Follow up
WORKSHEETS AS WE FORGIVE THOSE, PEACE IN OUR WORLD

Glossary
CONTRITION, PENANCE, ABSOLUTION, FIRM PURPOSE OF AMENDMENT, REMORSE, REPENTANCE.

— 5 Leadership in the Church —
Jesus calls his Disciples

Read how Jesus called his first five followers:

As Jesus walked along the shore of Lake Galilee, he saw two fishermen, Simon and his brother Andrew, catching fish with a net. Jesus said to them, *"Come with me, and I will teach you to catch people."* At once they left their nets and went with him. He went a little farther on and saw two other brothers, James and John, the sons of Zebedee. They were in their boat getting their nets ready. As soon as Jesus saw them, he called them; they left their father Zebedee in the boat with the hired men and went with Jesus. ...He went out again to the shore of the lake... and as he was walking on he saw Levi the son of Alphaeus, sitting by the customs house, and he said to him, *"Follow me"*. And he got up and followed him. *(Mk 1:16-20, 2:13-14)*

Jesus calls Simon (Peter) and Andrew.

Whom did Jesus call as his disciples?
He called ordinary people who were busy earning a living. There was nothing on the outside that would tell you these men were special. The four fishermen were hardworking men. Levi (or Matthew) collected taxes. Other people did not like him. He worked for the Romans, who had taken over the lands of the Jews.

Why did Jesus call disciples?
Jesus had come to set up God's Kingdom. He wanted to change the whole world. He needed people to help him in his work. These people he would teach so that they could carry his message to the whole world.

What did he say when he called them?
He said, **'Follow me'**. There was no time spent arguing or persuading. He just gave them a simple command.

What did they do when called?
They left everything and followed him.

What did Jesus see in these men?
He saw potential; he saw what the disciples could be with his help and guidance. Read the story below.

A Story
One day a famous sculptor had a large block of marble delivered. A little boy stood by as the block was unloaded. He watched the sculptor get to work. At various times when the sculptor was busy on the block the boy would pass by. At last the sculptor had finished what he was doing and covered over his work with a large cloth ready for the grand unveiling. A crowd gathered as the cloth was lifted from the finished sculpture. The boy, pushing through the crowd, saw what the sculptor had produced from the block of marble. It was a magnificent figure of a lion. Amazed, the boy asked the sculptor, 'How did you know there was a lion in that block of marble?'

In the same way, the disciples seemed ordinary men to other people. Jesus saw what the disciples could be after he had finished 'working on them'.

Activities

1. Read again the scripture and notes on the previous page. Answer the following in one sentence each.

A. When Jesus called his first disciples
(i) they were busy working?
(ii) they were waiting for him to call?
(iii) they ignored his call?

B. Jesus called his first disciples
(i) in Nazareth?
(ii) by the shores of Lake Galilee?
(iii) in Jerusalem?

C. Jesus' first disciples
(i) were very well educated people?
(ii) were well known for being religious?
(iii) seemed like ordinary working people?

D. When Jesus called the men to follow him, they
(i) asked for time to think about it?
(ii) left everything and followed him?
(iii) promised they would follow him later?

E. Jesus said to the fishermen that he would
(i) like to learn to fish?
(ii) give them a better life?
(iii) teach them to catch people?

F. Jesus called disciples to be with him because
(i) he felt lonely by himself?
(ii) he wanted workers for God's kingdom?
(iii) he wanted them to have an easier life?

2. Jesus called busy people.
(a) Re-read the scripture on the previous page.

(b) What were each of the five men doing before being called?

(c) Why did Jesus choose ordinary working men rather than educated religious experts?

Extension

3. Famous rock stars, film stars and professional footballers attract their followers or 'disciples'.

Famous people often attract large crowds of followers.

Write down three main differences between being a follower of Jesus and being a follower of a famous sporting, music or film personality.

Glossary

DISCIPLE.

Meet the Disciples

Jesus and twelve of his disciples at the last supper.

Read about the twelve people specially chosen to share their lives with Jesus.

Then Jesus went up a hill and called to himself the men he wanted. They came to him, and he chose twelve, whom he named apostles. "I have chosen you to be with me," he told them. "I will also send you out to preach, and you will have authority to drive out demons." These are the twelve he chose: Simon (Jesus gave him the name Peter); James and his brother John, the sons of Zebedee (Jesus gave them the name Boanerges, which means "Men of Thunder"); Andrew, Philip, Bartholomew, Matthew, Thomas, James son of Alphaeus, Thaddaeus, Simon the Patriot, and Judas Iscariot, who betrayed Jesus. *(Mk 3:13-19)*

Name: Simon

Family: Son of Jonah

Age: Older than John, a married man

Job: Fisherman

Home: Galilee

Other details: Jesus called this disciple Peter, which means **'rock'**. He was made the leader of the early Church, the first Pope. He was a spokesman for the other disciples. Sometimes his words got him into trouble. Jesus told him to **'feed my sheep'** by which he meant **'look after my followers'**. He was executed in Rome by the Emperor Nero many years later.

Name: John

Family: Son of Zebedee

Age: A very young man.

Job: Worked as fisherman in family business

Home: Galilee

Other details: This disciple was often chosen to be with Jesus at special times. He and his brother, James, were nicknamed **'Men of Thunder'**, perhaps because of their fiery tempers. John was especially loved by Jesus; he was beside Jesus at the Last Supper; he was with Mary at the foot of the cross. Later on, the Spirit guided him to write a Gospel and Letters for the New Testament.

Name: Levi or Matthew

Family: Son of Alphaeus

Age: Not known

Job: Tax Collector

Home: Galilee

Other details: There are few other details to give. After Jesus had ascended to heaven, Matthew was guided by the Spirit to write a Gospel.

Jesus spent the whole night in prayer before he chose these 12 men from a larger group of followers. These ordinary men would help him in his mission. They would also be leaders in the Church after Jesus ascended to heaven.

Activities

1. (a) Write a list of the 12 disciples.

(b) Write:
(i) the extra names that Jesus gave to some of the disciples.

(ii) what these extra names mean.

(c) Write down what Jesus told these 12 men when he called them together.

(d) Which disciple betrayed Jesus?

Research

2. Choose either **(a)** or **(b)**.

(a) Why twelve? Find out why Jesus chose 12 disciples.

Write up your findings in your own words.

(b) The 12 disciples have their own symbols.

Find out and explain in your own words the symbols of any 2 disciples.

Glossary

ASCEND, VOCATION, GALILEE, PREACH.

Follow Me!

What does *'follow me'* mean? At first, it means walk with me and go where I go. The disciples had to be with Jesus, listen to his words and see what he did. But this was so that they could learn from him. Disciple means **'learner'**. Jesus wanted his disciples to learn from him so that they could *become* like him. Before Jesus ascended to heaven, he sent out the disciples to preach the Gospel to all the world. The disciples were now apostles. Apostle means **'one who is sent out'**.

So, to sum up, 'follow me' means

- be with me,
- learn from me,
- become like me,
- be 'another me' in the world.

In others' eyes the disciples were not

- holy people.
- really well educated people.
- wealthy people.
- powerful people.

Jesus wanted his disciples to be like little children, *full of trust, joy, love, humility -* and *willing to learn.*

Activities

1. Design an acrostic using the word **'Disciples'**. Include in your acrostic what you have learnt about them.

2. Imagine you are Simon working on the shores of Lake Galilee. You are with a group near Jesus. Jesus looks at you for a while and says to you, **'Follow me.'** You are shocked; you don't know how to answer. A number of doubts come into your head. What's running through your mind? How are you going to answer?

(a) Divide a page in two, on one side copy the doubts from the thought bubble below. Add one more doubt to your own list.

(a) Choose appropriate answers from the other bubble to correspond with the doubts you have listed. Write them in on the other side of your page.

Doubts
"But what if I haven't got what it takes?"
"But I'm not very well educated."
"But I'm not ready."
"But what if you change your mind about me?"

Answers from Jesus
"I've chosen you, and I won't change my mind."
"There will never be a better time than now."
"I know you better than you know yourself; I know what you can do with my help."
"I will teach you all you need to know. As my disciple I want you to learn from me."

Glossary

APOSTLE.

Sharing his Mission

Jesus wanted his followers to share his mission. He wanted them to bring his love and mercy to the people in Palestine. At one time he sent them out in groups of two to the villages around. This would help the disciples to get ready for the time when they would carry Jesus' love and mercy to the whole world. Read the story of how Jesus sent out his disciples.

Then Jesus went to the villages round there, teaching the people. He called the twelve disciples together and sent them out two by two. He gave them authority over the evil spirits and ordered them, "Don't take anything with you on your journey except a stick - no bread, no beggar's bag, no money in your pockets. Wear sandals, but don't carry an extra shirt." He also said, "Wherever you are welcomed, stay in the same house until you leave that place. If you come to a town where people do not welcome you or will not listen to you, leave it and shake the dust off your feet. That will be a warning to them!"

So they went out and preached that people should turn away from their sins. They drove out many demons, and rubbed oil on many sick people and healed them.
(See Mk 6:7-13)

Activities

1. Jesus gave his disciples clear orders about how to travel and what to do.
Copy and complete the tables.

To take	Not to take
one pair of sandals	bread money

Do	Don't
travel in pairs preach	waste time with villages that don't want to know.

2. If Jesus had advertised for disciples in the **"Lakeside Times"**, what details would have to be included? Design his advert with details about:

- Qualifications needed,
- Personal qualities needed,
- Duties expected,
- Pay offered (if any),
- How to apply,
- Anything else you think necessary.

3. Read John's letter home.

To: Family of Zebedee
Galilee Heights

Dear All,
Sorry I did not write sooner. We've been so busy. You remember how worried you were when Jesus sent us out with no supplies? Well, you needn't have worried. Because we had no supplies we could set off straight away, we could travel quickly, and we were not mugged at any time. We had nothing worth stealing. Mind you, Jesus did allow us a stick to speed us up on the rocky paths. Travelling from village to village has been an amazing experience. The people gave us everything we needed, and because Jesus told us to stay at one place in each village people knew where to find us. We didn't waste our time with villages who wouldn't listen; we moved on as Jesus commanded. You'd never believe the power of Jesus' name. Evil was defeated and sicknesses were healed by using his name. Many people said they were sorry for their past sins and wanted to make a new start. It's been good to have some company on the roads. I'm with Matthew while James went off with Judas. Matthew's been brilliant. I was worried that he couldn't survive without the money he used to have, but he's not a bit bothered. I must go now. My love to all the family.
John
P.S. Hope the fishing business is going well. Jesus told me that you would get along fine without James and me.

(a) Why was Jesus' advice about what to take and not to take so helpful?

(b) Why was Jesus' advice about what to do and not to do so helpful?

Simon Peter

In the gospels, Simon Peter's name comes up more often than that of any other disciple. Why is this? There is a crucial scene in the gospels. Jesus and his disciples are walking along a path. Jesus asked his disciples who people thought he was. The disciples can easily answer this. They say that people think he is John the Baptist, Elijah or another prophet.

Then Jesus asks another question of the disciples: "Who do *you* say that I am?" This testing question seems to have silenced the disciples until Simon Peter spoke up...

Picture of St Peter by the famous artist Rubens.

'You are the Christ,' he said 'the Son of the living God'.
Jesus replied, 'Simon son of Jonah, you are a happy man! Because it was not flesh and blood that revealed this to you but my Father in heaven. So I now say to you: You are Peter and on this rock I will build my Church. And the gates of the underworld can never hold out against it. I will give you the keys to the Kingdom of heaven: whatever you bind on earth shall be considered bound in heaven; whatever you loose on earth shall be considered loosed in heaven.' (Mt 16:15-20)

As you study his progress think about the following:

- Did Simon live up to Jesus' hopes and expectations?

- Did he follow Jesus more closely than the others?

- Did he always understand what Jesus wanted?

- Did he always set the other disciples a good example?

- Did he stand by Jesus when things got rough?

- Did Jesus change his mind about Peter being the leader of the 12?

- Did Jesus know what Peter was like?

Jesus had high hopes of Simon the fisherman. Look at his progress in some of the pictures on the next page.

Peter's Progress

1. He was one of the first disciples to be called.

2. Jesus called him the Rock - Peter or Cephas.

3. He said that he would build his Church on this rock.

4. He gave him the keys to the Kingdom of Heaven.

5. Jesus prayed for Simon Peter so that he would have strong faith.

6. After Jesus' arrest, Peter denied three times that he even knew Jesus.

7. After Jesus' death Simon went back to fishing. The risen Jesus came back to him.

8. Jesus told him to look after his followers.

Activities

1. Write down the following statements and put **TRUE** or **FALSE** at the end of them.

(There is a Bible reference clue for each one.)

(a) Simon was called Peter by his parents.
(Clue Mark 3:16-19)

(b) Simon was a fisherman before he was a disciple. **(Clue Luke 5:1-8)**

(c) Simon was very quiet and never spoke up when he was with Jesus.
(Clue Matthew 14:25-31, Matthew 18:21-22)

(d) Simon was one of the three disciples Jesus took with him at special times.
**(Clue Mark 5:36-39, Mark 9:2-8,
Mark 14:32-34)**

(e) Simon always understood what Jesus meant. **(Clue Matthew 15:13-18)**

(f) Simon said that Jesus was the Messiah (Christ). **(Clue Matthew 16:13-19)**

(g) Simon made a promise to Jesus that he couldn't keep. **(Clue Luke 22:33-34)**

(h) Because he let Jesus down Simon was not allowed to continue being the leader of the disciples. **(Clue John 21:15-17)**

(i) Simon did very little to spread the Good News of the Resurrection. **(Clue Acts 2:4-16)**

Extension

2. (a) Imagine that Simon Peter is being examined by lawyers in a court. The court wants to judge whether Peter should still be the leader of the Church.

Peter awaits trial in prison

This is what the prosecution lawyers say:

"Your honour, we find the defendant, Simon of Galilee, unfit to be leader of the Church. It's clear to us that he is an unstable character, saying one thing then doing another. He tends to speak first and then think later, the mark of a fool. Early on he admitted to Jesus that he was a sinner. He begged Jesus to leave him. Jesus didn't. What was Jesus' reward? To be rejected three times by one he thought was a true friend. How can someone who let Jesus down so badly now be leader of his Church? Your honour, we rest our case."

(b) You are the lawyer leading the defence of Peter. Write down your statement to the court.

Pentecost

Luke wrote two books of the New Testament: Book 1 was Luke's Gospel, and Book 2 was the Acts of the Apostles. At the end of Luke's Gospel Jesus said goodbye to his followers. Before he ascended to heaven he promised them that power from on high would come down on them. Jesus kept his promise. The Acts of the Apostles tells us about this.

> Suddenly there was a noise from the sky which sounded like a strong wind blowing, and it filled the whole house where they were sitting. Then they saw what looked like tongues of fire which spread out and touched every person there. They were all filled with the Holy Spirit and began to talk in other languages, as the Spirit enabled them to speak. *(Acts 2:2-4)*

The Time
The Jewish Feast of Pentecost, 50 days after Passover.

The Place
Jerusalem.

The Situation
The followers of Jesus have met together in one room to pray. Among these followers are the apostles, others who knew Jesus along with Mary, the mother of Jesus. They are waiting for the power from on high to come down on them. They are waiting for Jesus to keep his promise.

The Event
The Holy Spirit descends in great power like a fiery breath from heaven. A flame settles on the head of each person. This shows that they have been filled with the Holy Spirit.

The Result
The apostles are like new men. They can preach that Jesus is risen, and people of different languages can understand them. The crowd are dazzled. Some think the apostles are drunk - but it's only 9 in the morning. By the end of the day about 3000 believe and are baptised in Jesus' name.

Looking Back
That Pentecost day was the Church's birthday. On that day the Church was born for all to see.

Activities

1. A big block of words has been split into four smaller blocks and mixed up.

Can you write out the words in the correct way?

went out to preach. of many nations and nt. They all could the apostles said. ved in Jesus on the s born.	Then the apostles There were people languages presen understand what 3000 people believ day the Church was
the Holy Spirit is cts of the Apostles. he Spirit were wind pirit filled the minds ho were in the room.	The Descent of described in the A The symbols of tⁱ and fire. The Hoy and hearts of all wⁱ

2. Draw a line across your page. Mark and label on your line the following days in the correct order.

Pentecost Day
• fifty days after Passover.

Resurrection Day
• the day after Passover.

Ascension Day
• traditionally ten days before Pentecost.

Good Friday
• the day before Passover when Jesus died.

Passover
• the greatest feast in the Jewish Year recalling the freedom of the Israelites from slavery in Egypt.

3. Draw a flame to represent the Holy Spirit.

(a) Around the flame write words that describe the effect of the Holy Spirit on the apostles.

You might want to use the word bank.

(b) In the darkness further from the flame write what was '**driven out**' by the light of the Holy Spirit.

You might want to use the word bank.

Word Bank

fear   hesitation   regret

worry   hope   enthusiasm

joy   uncertainty

peace   courage

Activities

4. Read the following '**interrogation**'. Imagine you are Simon Peter. Answer the last question asked by the interrogators.

Officials question Peter on the events of Pentecost.

Thank you for agreeing to be questioned. You are not under arrest, and may leave at any time you wish. Do you understand this?
Yes.

Well, let's get started, shall we? You are Simon, the one they call Peter, the Rock?
I am.

Tell us why you're called the Rock.
Jesus gave me that name. He said I am the rock on which he will build his Church.

Do you see yourself as a rock, Simon?
How I see myself is not important. What's important is how Jesus sees me. He chose me; I didn't choose myself.

Forgive us for bringing this up, Simon, but we have witnesses who say that last Passover you denied three times that you knew this Jesus. Surely a 'Rock' does not behave in this way?
You're right. I was a coward. I bitterly regret what I said and did the night before he died. But Jesus forgave me.

When, exactly, did Jesus forgive you?
I saw him after he rose from the dead and he said...

Hold it right there. Rose from the dead, you say?

That's right. Three days after he was crucified, he rose again, just as he said he would.

You really expect us to believe that a man who died the shameful death on the cross could actually rise again?
Yes. You should all believe - and be baptised in the name of Jesus.

Well, I'm afraid we'll have to pass up on your kind offer. I want to turn now to the extraordinary commotion of Pentecost, a few days back. You and others began to spread these stories of 'the risen Jesus' among the people.
Yes.

Why did you wait from Passover to Pentecost to proclaim this so-called truth?
Jesus told us to wait until the Holy Spirit came down on us.

Look, Simon, you're asking us to believe an awful lot of stories. Our sources tell us that when your Jesus was executed you and those others ran off. We also have evidence to suggest that you've all been meeting behind closed doors and keeping your heads down.
That's true.

Tell us, what exactly turned a group of cowards who met in secret into a group of fearless preachers. Had you been drinking new wine?

Follow up
WORKSHEETS SPIRIT OF UNITY, EARLY CHRISTIANS

Glossary
ASCEND, DESCEND.

Pope and Bishops

Some time after Pentecost, Peter went to Antioch, a great city to the north of Jerusalem. He was Bishop of Antioch for a few years. Then he went to Rome, the centre of the Empire, and was Bishop of Rome.

When the Emperor Nero began persecuting Christians in 64 AD, Peter and Paul were both killed. Paul was beheaded, while Peter, it is said, was crucified upside down.

The Church in Rome became the most important Church for other Christians. It was in Rome where the two greatest leaders of the early Church, Peter and Paul, were martyred.

Some Popes past and present.

There have been over two hundred and sixty popes from Peter to the present day.

Bishops

The apostles passed on the authority Jesus gave them. They *laid hands* on other men and called down the Holy Spirit on them. These men were called *bishops* and looked after the Church in a certain place. These bishops laid hands on other men to make new bishops. That is why bishops are successors of the apostles. They have received the same Spirit and duties of the apostles. There are many bishops throughout the world today. Bishops look after the Church in a certain place called a diocese.

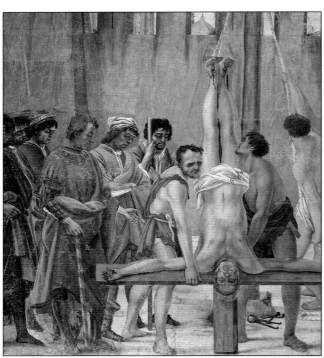

The Martyrdom of St Peter.

Pope

Many others came after Peter as Bishop of Rome. Later, the Bishop of Rome was often called Pope, a word meaning 'father'. Catholics believe him to be Peter's successor. This means that he has the same task of leading the whole Church.

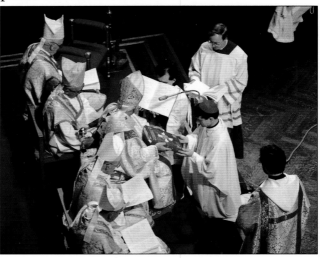

The ordination of a Bishop.

Activities

1. Read again the notes on the last page. Now try to write the correct explanation next to each of these.

Simon Peter	– successors of the apostles
Pope	– the Church in a certain area looked after by a bishop
Diocese	– Catholics believe that he leads the Church on earth
Bishops	– Catholics believe that he was the first pope

2. (a) Write down the three most important ways in which a shepherd looks after a flock of sheep.

(b) A bishop is meant to be a shepherd to 'his flock' - the Church in his diocese. Do you think 'shepherd' is a good word to describe a bishop? Explain your answer.

A bishop is responsible for the people in his diocese.

Research

3. If a bishop has visited your school or parish, you might see him wearing a **mitre** and carrying a **crosier**.

Archbishop Cormac Murphy-O'Connor with his mitre and crosier.

(a) Find out what a mitre and crosier are.

(b) Write up your findings, explaining what they symbolise.

Glossary

POPE, SUCCESSOR.

Some titles of the Pope

Pope

'Pope' means father. This shows that the Pope must be like a loving father to God's People on earth.

Holy Father

Again, this title shows how the Pope must be like a loving father.

Bishop of Rome

The Pope is the Bishop of Rome. Peter was Bishop of Rome. The Pope is a successor of one apostle, Peter. Other bishops are successors of the apostles as a group.

Vicar of Christ

A 'vicar' acts in the place of someone. Catholics believe that the Pope is the Vicar of Christ because he acts in Christ's place as Head of the Church on earth. This shows that the Pope's authority comes from Jesus Christ. The Pope has no authority of his own.

Servant of the Servants of God

Those who work in the Church, especially bishops and priests, are servants of God. The Pope is even more of a servant. Since he has to serve the whole Church, he is the servant of the servants of God.

Activities

1. A big block of words has been broken into four smaller blocks and mixed up. Can you write out the words in the correct way.

₃ successors of the means they have spirit by laying on ᵢen. These men had rs like the apostles. ᵢlled bishops. They ᵢh in a certain area	ent day. Bishops arₑ 12 apostles. This received the same ₃ hands on suitable m then the job of leadₑ These men were ca look after the churc called a diocese.
essor of Peter. Like ᵢe Bishop of Rome. ob of leading the word 'pope' means e been over 260 eter up to the pres-	The Pope is the succ Peter, The Pope is th He has the same j whole Church. The ᵥ 'father'. There havₑ popes from Simon Pₑ

2. When Pope Leo XIII died in 1903, a newspaper in England wrote:

> 'The great keys have now been surrendered, and their weight, carried for so many years with courage, has been lifted at last.'

(a) What did the newspaper mean by the '**great keys**'?

(b) What did the newspaper mean by the '**weight**' of these keys?

3. In Rome there is a small State called the Vatican. The Pope is based there. Below is the Vatican's crest, made up of a tiara and two keys, with the Pope's personal emblem.

Find out what you can about the symbols in the crest and write up your findings.

Follow up
WORKSHEET **SOME POPES & COUNCILS**

Glossary
VICAR.

6 The Church's Mission
Images of the Church

The word to describe *Church* in the Greek (and Latin) was **'ecclesia'** which means **'assembly'** - the assembly of God's People. The Church is the people God gathered together.

If you want a definition:
the Church is the People of God united to God and to each other by the Holy Spirit in baptism.

It is important to remember that when God calls his People, he calls them *together*. So the People of God are joined to God and to each other. See the pictures on the right for an explanation.

Images of the Church

There are various images or ways of picturing the Church, for example:

- a building made of **'living stones'** - with Christ as the cornerstone;

- the Body of Christ, - with Christ as the Head of the Body;

- a sheepfold - with Jesus as the Good Shepherd.

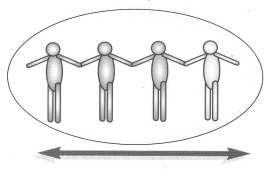

God

The Church does not just mean being close to each other with God above us.

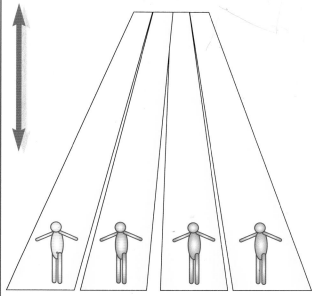

God

The Church does not mean trying to be close to God but not close to each other.

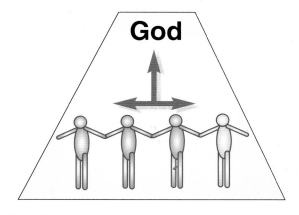

God

The Church means being united with God and with each other.

Activities

1. Join the sentences together correctly and write them down.

The Church means being united with God	but not close to others.

The Church does not mean trying to be close to God	with God above us.

The Church does not mean being close to each other	and with each other.

2. Look at the pictures on the right. Each one is an image of the Church.

    (a) Write down the name of each image.

    (b) Write down one different thing that each image tells you about the Church (for example, image A suggests leadership and guidance).

    (c) Which image most helps you to understand what the Church is?

    Explain your answer.

Extension

3. Imagine a community of 300 worshippers at Mass at St. James' Catholic Church. Imagine that there is also a crowd of 300 people shopping in a nearby shopping centre.

    (a) Apart from the difference in place, what would you say are the main differences between the community of 300 and the crowd of 300?

    (b) Explain one way in which the worshippers show they are a community during the Mass?

Image A

Image B

Image C

Glossary

CHURCH, CORNERSTONE, SHEEPFOLD, ASSEMBLY, CONGREGATION.

Four Marks of the Church

In the Nicene Creed there is the line:

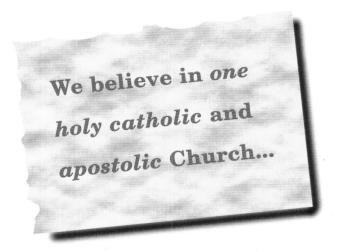

We believe in one holy catholic and apostolic Church...

The words - *one, holy, catholic, apostolic* - are called the **four marks of the Church**. Without these marks the Church cannot be. These marks are features of the Church always, whatever the century, wherever the place, whatever the situation.

On the surface, Church communities might look very different. A Church Mission in Tanzania will seem very different to a parish in inner London. An underground Church community in China seems totally unlike a peaceful parish in the countryside of England. And yet deep down they are all expressions of the Church, since they are a part of the one, holy, catholic and apostolic Church. *What do these 'four marks of the Church' mean?*

One

Since there is one Christ, there is one Church, which is his Body. The Church has one Lord, one faith, one baptism and one Spirit. Jesus prayed that all his followers would be one as he and his Father are one.

Holy

God is holy. Christ came to call all people to be holy. The Church is holy because it is united with Christ, who is both God and man.

Catholic

Catholic means *'universal'* or *'whole'*. The Church is catholic because Jesus gives the Church the whole way for people to be saved, and the Church has the task of reaching out to the whole world with the message of Jesus.

Apostolic

The Church grew from the witness of the apostles about the risen Jesus. The faith of the Church is handed on through the apostles and their successors, the bishops, under the leadership of the Pope.

Note that

- *'One'* does not mean *'exactly the same everywhere you go'*. The Church in different countries mirrors some of the special features of those countries. Deep down, the Church is still united by the same Spirit, which gives her one faith and worship.

- *'Holy'* does not mean that there are no sinners in the Church. Members of the Church are human and so have the weaknesses of humans. The Church is more a *'hospital for sinners'* than a *'hotel for the good'*.

Activities

1. Try to join the four broken pieces below. Write down what was written on them.

the whole truth from e handed on through heir successors, the ;h must preach the s of all times.	Church has received Christ, which must b the apostles and th bishops. The Churc Gospel to all peoples
, holy, catholic and ne, holy, catholic and four marks of the is the one Body of e Christ is holy. The	'We believe in one, apostolic Church.' Or apostolic are the Church. The Church Christ, holy because

2. Write down the following sentences and put a **'true'** or **'false'** after each to show what Catholics believe.

(a) Because the Church is one, there are no differences allowed from one place to another.

(b) Because the Church is holy, there can be no sinners in the Church.

(c) Because the Church is catholic, it must reach out to all people of all times.

(d) Because the Church is apostolic, it has bishops to hand on the faith of the apostles.

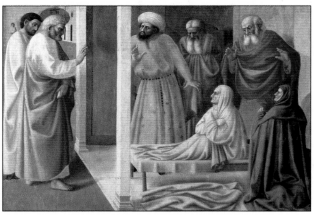

Life in the early Church.
St Peter healing a sick woman.

Extension

3. Read this description of the early Church from the Acts of the Apostles.

The early Christian community: These remained faithful to the teaching of the apostles, to the brotherhood, to the breaking of bread and to the prayers. The many miracles and signs worked through the apostles made a deep impression on everyone. The faithful all lived together and owned everything in common; they sold their goods and possessions and shared out the proceeds among themselves according to what each one needed. They went as a body to the temple every day but met in their houses for the breaking of bread; they shared their food gladly and generously; they praised God and were looked up to by everyone. Day by day the Lord added to their community those destined to be saved. (Acts 2:42-47)

What evidence can you take from this passage to show any one of the four marks of the Church?

Explain your answer.

Glossary

FOUR MARKS OF THE CHURCH, HOLY, CATHOLIC, APOSTOLIC, CREED.

The Mission of the Church

Because the Church is *catholic* and *apostolic*, she must reach out to the whole of humankind with the message of the apostles. At the end of Matthew's Gospel, Jesus gave his apostles their mission.

"Go and make disciples of all nations; baptise them in the name of the Father and of the Son and of the Holy Spirit, and teach them to follow the commands I gave you. And know that I am with you always; yes, to the end of time." *(Mt 28:19-20)*

This mission is also the mission of the Church to the world. For the small band of apostles this mission must have seemed like 'mission impossible'. However, with God all things are possible.

The mission of the Church to the world is:

- **TO GO OUT to the ends of the earth.**

- **TO BAPTISE people into the Church.**

- **TO TEACH the commands of Christ.**

The Church began in Jerusalem and in a few decades spread quickly throughout the Roman Empire. Soon the Church reached the great centre of the Empire: Rome itself. As well as to Rome, missionaries went to many other parts of the Roman Empire.

They often faced misunderstanding. Sometimes they were beaten up or killed. Sometimes Christians had to meet together in secret places. At other times the Church was left in peace.

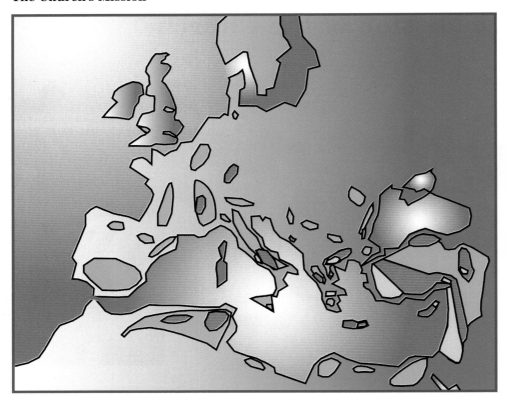

The spread of the Church in the first three centuries of Christianity

first century

second century

third century

Activities

1. (a) What is the Mission of the Church to the world?

(b) Who makes this Mission possible?

2. Look at the map above. Draw a line across a page in your exercise book. Without worrying about dates, mark with a cross on the line the following events - in the correct order:

(a) when Christianity began.
(b) when Christianity reached Britain.
(c) when Christianity reached Rome.
(d) when Christianity reached North Africa.
(e) when Christianity reached Spain.

3. Read the story of Fr Damien, a missionary to the Hawaiian Islands. Then:

(a) Read again Jesus' final instructions to his disciples. Explain how Fr Damien followed the commands of Jesus.

(b) What do you think eventually happened to Fr Damien?

A Story

Father Damien de Veuster, a Belgian Priest, was born in 1840. He volunteered to travel to the Hawaiian Islands as a missionary. In those days Hawaii was very different from what you would see today.

The Islands had been visited by a terrible wave of leprosy (Hansen's disease). With no treatment this disease disfigured the bodies and faces of victims and caused great pain. Because the disease was contagious, a ruler of the Hawaiian Islands had rounded up all those suffering from the disease, including children, and put them on a lonely island, Molokai.

There the sufferers were left to fend for themselves. Those who only had small signs of the disease tended to beat and steal from those who were weaker. The place was filled with despair. Those abandoned in Molokai must have felt abandoned by God. God, however, sent Father Damien to be a priest among them. A priest to bring the Gospel to them, to care for them, to give them the sacraments, to give them hope and to help make their lives better. He spent the rest of his life in this work.

The Church Spreads

Paul, the Apostle of the Gentiles

Paul was one of the greatest missionaries of the early Church. He founded (set up) Christian communities in a number of cities of the Roman Empire. He worked hard to bring Gentiles (non-Jews) into the Church.

He had a dream in which a person from Macedonia (near Greece) was calling him to bring the Gospel to them. His work in Europe and in Asia Minor (Turkey) was a great success. Read the snapshot of his life below.

Name:	Saul/Paul
Born:	about AD 10
Place:	Tarsus
Occupation:	Tent maker

Paul was born a Jew, and he took his faith very seriously. He became a Pharisee. At first, he hated the followers of Jesus and persecuted them. Then, after a dazzling vision of Jesus, he became a follower of Jesus. He spent a number of years in Arabia before returning to Jerusalem. He became a great preacher and leader in the early Church.

At first, Paul preached to the Jews in the cities of the Empire. Soon, he began preaching to Gentiles (people who are not Jews). With his companions Paul travelled by land and sea through the Empire. He never grew tired of preaching

the Gospel. He wrote letters to certain Christian communities. Many of these letters are in the New Testament.

When Nero began persecuting Christians, Paul was among the victims. He was beheaded in about AD 67.

Activities

1. Paul suffered much to spread the Gospel. Read **2 Corinthians 11:21-27**. How many times was Paul:

    (a) whipped? **(b)** beaten? **(c)** stoned?

    (d) shipwrecked?

2. What other dangers and hardships did Paul face?

3. Why do you think Paul was so successful as a missionary?

4. What example does St Paul give to Christian missionaries today?

Follow up: Christianity in the Roman Empire
WORKSHEETS
THE ROMAN WORLD,
A PERSECUTED CHURCH,
KEEPING IN TOUCH, PERSECUTION ENDS,
NEW MISSIONS

Glossary
PERSECUTE, PHARISEE.

Extension

5. Persecution of Christians has continued through the centuries.

(a) Read the story of Charles Lwanga and the martyrs of Uganda.

(b) Do you think Charles and his companions were asking for trouble by not living in total fear of the King?

(c) Charles told his executioner,

> "How happy I should be if you, too, would become a Christian."

The executioner laughed at this, but he did later ask to join the Church.

What do you think made him change his mind?

Names:	Charles Lwanga & Companions 22 Martyrs of Uganda
Died:	1885-1887
Canonised:	1964

The King of Buganda had invited Catholic missionaries ('the praying ones') to return to his kingdom. When they did return, they found the work they had done earlier had come to blossom. They found a Christian community that prayed together and supported each other just as in the early Church. Charles Lwanga and others had become Christians and were faithful to the Gospel in spite of hardship. A plague had struck the Kingdom and they had gone out to help the sick without worrying about themselves.

Unfortunately, the young King became much harsher. He wanted all in his kingdom to fear him. The peaceful Christians didn't seem to live in any fear. He changed his mind about Christians and began to threaten them. He was determined to kill 'those who pray' as he called the Christians. He rounded them up and put them to cruel deaths one by one. Charles was burned to death, praying for the man who was killing him. Twenty one Catholic Ugandans died in a similar way.

The Church - Yesterday, Today, Always

The Church has grown and developed since the early days. However, in certain ways the Church is the same. Jesus is still present in the Church in the world today.

In the Church of today believers meet Jesus, his teaching and his mercy. They receive his forgiveness, strength and life in the Eucharist and other sacraments.

A New Testament writer said that Jesus is the same yesterday, today and forever. Since the Church is his Body, the Church is also the same yesterday, today, and right to the end of time.

The Church - yesterday, today, to the end of time

From the birth of the Church at Pentecost until today, the following things have always been important in Catholic life and worship:

Conversion
To join the Church, a person must still turn from sin to God.

Belief
That person must still accept the faith of the Church expressed in the *Creed*.

Eucharist
The Eucharist, or the Mass, is still the most important worship of the Church.

Stay together
The Holy Spirit unites Catholics all over the world. They accept the Church's faith, worship and moral teaching as coming from Jesus.

Pray together
The Mass is the great prayer of the Church. The Church prays together in other ways too, (e.g. the *Divine Office*).

Share together
'Share' means that the hopes, joys, pains and needs of the Church in one place should be felt by the whole Church.

Apostles
The Church is still led by the successors of Peter and the other apostles - the Pope and the other bishops.

Activities

1. Copy the table, putting in the details correctly.

Early Church	Catholic Church today	Both

Details
- a small, but growing, number of believers.
- about 1 billion believers.
- in small groups in cities around the Mediterranean Sea.
- to be found in every corner of the earth
- led by apostles or by elders who knew the apostles.
- led by the successors of the apostles celebrating the Eucharist.
- praying and sharing together.
- united by one Spirit, one faith and one baptism.

Glossary
DIVINE OFFICE, MORAL TEACHING.

Organisation in the Church

If you had an important mission to carry out, you would have to be organised in order to complete the task properly. The missionaries of the Church were organised. In all their various missions they left in place a way of organising the christian community.

In any particular country the Church is usually organised like this. There may be one or more *dioceses*, each looked after by a bishop. Each diocese is split into smaller areas called *deaneries*. The smallest Church community is the *parish*, with the local community and a parish priest. In countries where the Catholic communities are few and far between, parishes may be very large. A priest may often have to oversee a number of parishes.

See the picture below for further explanation.

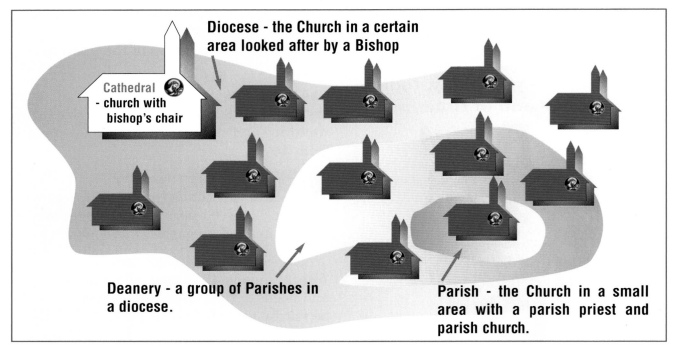

Diocese - the Church in a certain area looked after by a Bishop

Cathedral - church with bishop's chair

Deanery - a group of Parishes in a diocese.

Parish - the Church in a small area with a parish priest and parish church.

Activities

1. Fit each name with the right meaning and then write out each sentence.

Church	the church is a small area with a parish priest and parish church.
Deanery	the church in a certain area for which a Bishop is responsible.
Parish	- the main church in a diocese: it has the Bishop's chair in it.
Diocese	a group of parishes in a diocese.
Cathedral	the people of God.

Research

2. Use your skills of research to answer as many of the following questions about the Catholic Church in England and Wales.

  (a) What is the name of your diocese?
  (b) What is the name of the bishop?
  (c) Can you name three parishes connected with your school?
  (d) Who is the leader of the Catholic Church in England and Wales?
  (e) How many dioceses are there in England and Wales?
  (f) Why are some dioceses small in area whilst others are large?

Glossary
DIOCESE, DEANERY, PARISH, CATHEDRAL.

The Local Church

Here is part of a newsletter which you might find in any Catholic parish. This is a page of the newsletter for *The Holy Family Parish*.

The newsletter comes out every week and tells the parishioners of the times of Mass and of what's going on in the Holy Family Parish.

✚ Holy Family Newsletter ✚

Father David Johnson
Father Martin McDaniel

The Presbytery, St Augustine's Way, Shenfield, BA11 4QS

Tel: (01876) 546371 Fax: (01876) 645382

15th Sunday of the Year (A)

Vigil Mass	6.00 pm	Martin family
Sun 11th	9.00 am	Hart Family
	11.00 am	Joan Rogers
	5.00 pm	Rosary and Benediction

Mon 12th   **Feria**

Holy Mass	8.00 am	Francis Brady
Holy Mass	12.10 pm	Vincent D'Souza RIP

Tues 13th   **St Henry**

Holy Mass	8.00 am	Henry Brooks RIP

Wed 14th   **Feria**

Holy Mass	8.00 am	J. Boniek's intentions
Holy Mass	12.10 pm	Holy Souls

Thurs 15th   **St Bonaventure**

Holy Mass	8.00 am	Walters Family
Holy Mass	12.10 pm	Agnes Given RIP

Frid 16th   **Our Lady of Mt Carmel**
Exposition begins at 8.30 am

Holy Mass	8.00 am	B. Roundhay

Exposition ends at 7.00 pm
with Evening Prayer

Holy Mass	7.30 pm	J. Suarez RIP

Sat 17th   **Our Lady's Saturday**

Holy Mass	8.00 am	D. Zupanic's intentions
Vigil Mass	6.00 pm	
Confessions	10-10.30 am, 4-5 pm	

Next Sunday is the 16th Sunday of the Year

	Reader	Eucharistic Minister
Vigil	L. Dawes	F. Burgess, C D'Mello
9.00 am	J. Carlos	N. Domingues
11.00 am	H. Fitzhenry	S. Beinoras

Coffee
D. Selston, R. Lascelles

Planned Giving Counters
H. Fisher, B. Higgins, V. Brown

Church Cleaning
G Woodforde, A Prydchodko, A Hart

Flowers
J Czabo, D Brownlow, F Daly

RCIA
Are you interested in the Catholic Faith? Do you know of anyone who is interested or who would like to deepen their faith? If so, the parish RCIA is for you. The programme is a step by step introduction to the heart of the Catholic Faith. Those interested can be assured of a warm welcome and a stimulating series of talks and presentations. Next meeting is Wednesday 21st in the Parish Hall at 7.00 pm.

GARDEN PARTY
Saturday 17th July 2.00 pm - 4.30 pm Raffles.
Games. Fancy Goods

From the newsletter you can see how important it is for people in the parish to become involved with parish life. It is not just the priest's job to run everything.

The priest has a clear role in the parish: to preach the Word, to administer the sacraments, to visit the sick and to guide people in the Christian life. That's a busy enough schedule.

The people of the parish can and should help. Why? Because they have special abilities. The priest cannot be an expert in many areas needed for the smooth running of the parish. People in the parish show that they share in the mission of the Church by giving their time, energy and abilities to parish life.

Activities

1. Use the newsletter to study how parishioners stay in touch with others in the Church and how they try to reach out to the local community.

(a) Copy the spider diagram below and try to make connections by writing along the lines.

local people who are not Catholics

other people in the parish

people in the parish → They pray for each other. They worship together

poor people in the world

saints in heaven

parishioners who have died

(b) Are there other connections that you can make that are not in the diagram?

2. Have a quick read through the newsletter on the previous page.

(a) Look at all the different people involved in the life of the parish of **The Holy Family**.

Some parishioners wrap presents for the elderly at Christmas time.

(b) In what ways do parishioners (members of the Parish) help out in the parish?

Make a list. Aim to write six different ways.

3. Read the story below.

A Story

A priest was given a new parish. After a few months in the parish, he tried to organise a youth group, a choir, and a rota for visiting the lonely and housebound. To his dismay he found that the parishioners, didn't seem interested in anything except doing the bare minimum.

Anything extra - they didn't want to know. One Sunday, he read out a notice that the Church's funeral would be in a week's time. He said the body could be viewed before the burial.

Next Sunday, the people came to church curious to look in the coffin in the centre of the aisle. The priest solemnly opened the coffin and asked people to walk by silently and pay their respects to the dead Church. When each person looked inside the coffin, they saw a mirror and their own reflection in the mirror.

(a) Explain what you think is the main message of this story.

(b) Imagine what happened, and how things changed for the better. Write a paragraph.

Glossary

COMMITMENT, PARISHIONER, RCIA.

The Church Overseas

Farai's Story

Hello - or in my language Kwaziwai. My name is Farai. I am sixteen years old. I want to tell you about the Church in my home country of Zimbabwe. I live in a small village in the north of the country. Every day I rise before 5 a.m. to bathe in the river nearby. I have many jobs to do about the house, for example, collecting water, starting the fire to boil water, preparing sadza (a porridge made from maize), sweeping the yard, and so on. Sunday is a very special day for me. I have to finish all my chores before 7.30, when my mother and I leave to walk to the mission church, about 8 km away through the hills. On our way we meet others travelling from their village, all of us gathering together to worship God.

We arrive at the beautiful mission church an hour later. Already many of the women are there and we begin the singing. I am allowed to beat the big drum to keep the singing in time. There are many different beats and I have to make sure I know them.

Mass begins at 9 a.m. It is a joyful occasion. Hundreds of people, young and old from all the villages around are present. When we all sing together it seems like the roof is going to lift off the church.

At the offertory there is a procession of gifts; the people dance and sing in time to my drumming and bring up to the altar some of the things they grow: bananas, mangoes, okra, pumpkins, sweet potatoes. With these offerings the Church is able to help the poorer people with food.

During communion we all sing my favourite hymn: Mwari ngarumbidzwe kudenga - Let God in heaven be praised.

After Mass we continue singing and celebrating until about 11 am. Outside the church the people talk and laugh; the priests and deacons join them. The village children run around and play. Everybody is like one big family of God. This is what Church means to me.

Activities

1. Read Farai's story above.

(a) How important is Sunday worship for Farai? Explain your answer.

(b) Farai adds to the life of the Church by her gift for drumming.

What gifts could a young Catholic in Britain offer to the Church in their area?

2. The Greek and Latin word for Church is **Ecclesia**. It means '**assembly**' or '**gathering**'.

(a) Write one sentence from the story above that gets across the idea of gathering together.

(b) Copy and complete the table about the Church in different places.

Church in Zimbabwe	Church everywhere	Church in Britain
Drums used in singing.	The main day of worship is Sunday.	Organ often used with singing.

Aim to include at least three more rows to the table.

Extension

3. Write a letter to Farai to explain about the life and work of the Church in your area.

The Communion of Saints

These are lines from the Apostles' Creed:

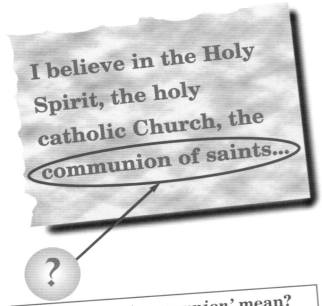

I believe in the Holy Spirit, the holy catholic Church, the communion of saints...

?

What does 'communion' mean?

What does 'communion of saints' mean?

Communion means 'complete union'. To believe in the 'communion of saints' is to believe that everyone in the Church is linked with one another. No-one in the Church is alone. A bell is not a bell if there is the smallest crack in it; the metal in the bell must be perfectly fused if it is to chime. Similarly, the Church is not the Church unless there is a union in the Holy Spirit of all its members, living and dead, with Jesus.

Catholics believe that there are three states of the Church:

- the Church on earth - the Church journeying to God.

- the Church in triumph - the saints in heaven with God.

- the Church still suffering - the holy souls in purgatory being made clean for heaven.

These three states are linked:

- believers on earth can help each other by prayers and support;

- the saints in heaven pray for us;

- the holy souls in purgatory need our prayers, but also pray for us too.

Activities

1. Explain in your own words what is meant by
   (a) the Communion of Saints,
   (b) the three states of the Church.

Research

2. The Feast of All Saints and the Feast of All Souls are on two days next to each other.
   (a) Write down the dates of these two feast days.
   (b) Why do you think these two feast days are together?

Glossary
COMMUNION OF SAINTS, PURGATORY.

Saints

Saints come in all shapes and sizes, from every corner of the earth. Some have died young, others have lived long lives. Some have been killed for their Christian faith, others have not. Some have been priests or religious, others wives, husbands or unmarried. Some have been very well educated, others could not read or write. Some have travelled far and wide, others have stayed in one place.

> ### All saints:
>
> - wished to serve God and others.
>
> - did not give up trying, even when they made mistakes.
>
> - were real people with the usual hopes and difficulties of life to face.
>
> - lived joyful lives.
>
> - show how anyone can be a saint by his or her example.

What is a saint?

Do this quick quiz before you go any further. Chose (a) or (b).

1.(a) *All Christians are called to be saints.*
(b) Some Christians are called to be saints.

2.(a) *Being a saint means being 'truly yourself' as God made you to be.*
(b) Being a saint means being 'someone else', someone who seems holier than you.

3.(a) *You can be holy whilst living an ordinary life in the world.*
(b) You cannot be holy and live an ordinary life in the world.

4.(a) *Being a saint usually means doing little things well for love of God.*
(b) Being a saint usually means doing 'big things' for God.

5.(a) *Some saints are well known, other saints are known only to God.*
(b) Saints are only those people with a St. in front of their name.

6.(a) *Saints are ordinary people with ordinary faults and temptations to cope with.*
(b) Saints are special people who don't have the faults and temptations of ordinary people.

Father Damien de Veuster.

7. (a) *Great sinners can become great saints.*
(b) Great saints were never great sinners.

8. (a) *Saints learn to love God and their neighbour.*
(b) Saints learn to follow rules carefully.

> ## Activities
>
> **1.** Copy and complete the acrostic below.
>
>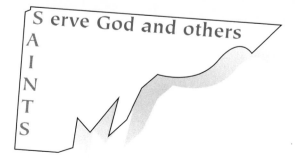
>
> **S** erve God and others
> **A**
> **I**
> **N**
> **T**
> **S**
>
> **2. (a)** Put a '**Saint**' in front of your first name.
>
> **(b)** Write a short story of your life, a life in which you became a saint.

More Saints

When the Catholic Church canonises a person, that person is being recognised as a saint. It means that the person is a very good example of how to live a Christian life. It means that the person is with God in heaven and, like all the friends of God, will pray for us still on our way to God. There are also many other saints that are known only to God. Read the following snapshots of the lives of some saints.

**Maximilian Kolbe
1894-1941
Poland
Canonised in
1982**

The scene was Auschwitz in 1941. A prisoner had just escaped, and so the Nazis dragged out ten prisoners to be executed. One of them, Francis Gajowniszec, begged to be spared because of his family. At this point another prisoner volunteered to take his place, saying: "I am a Catholic Priest." The Commandant allowed the substitution. The priest, Fr Kolbe, and nine others were condemned to die in the starvation cell. For two weeks without food or water Fr Kolbe prayed with the men, though at the end there were four left - Fr Kolbe among them. These were finished off with an injection of poison. Fr Kolbe died on his knees in prayer...

**Gemma Galgani
1878-1903
Italy
Died aged 25
Canonised in 1940**

She was pretty; she was bright; she was popular. Unfortunately her parents died early. Aged 19 Gemma found herself in charge of a family of 7 brothers and sisters. The family was in debt, the debt collectors taking away anything of value on the day of her father's funeral. How would she cope with no money, no parents, poor health and younger ones needing care? All she had was a simple, deep life of prayer, and that would be enough...

**Charles de
Foucauld
1858-1916
France/Algeria
Declared Venerable
in 1978**

Born into a wealthy family, Charles was a 'wild child'. He was expelled from school, and then went on to join the French army. He had a terrible reputation, loving to shock others by his behaviour. In his own words, he was bigheaded, vain, anti-religious and very sinful. He had rejected God, but God hadn't rejected him...

Research & write-up

Choose another saint to research. Include:

- a brief story of their life.

- why they are a good example to others.

- the date of their feast day.

- any other interesting details.

Glossary

CANONISATION, VENERABLE, BEATIFY.

Glossary

ABEL - Adam and Eve's son; he was murdered by his brother, Cain.

ABSOLUTION - complete forgiveness of sins.

ABSOLVE - to forgive completely.

ACT OF CHARITY - an act of kindness to someone else.

ACT OF CONTRITION - a prayer of sorrow to God.

ACTS OF THE APOSTLES - the fifth book of the NT.

ADAM - the first man.

ADORATION - adoring God as the Creator; and in the Blessed Sacrament.

ADVENT - four week season of prayer, penance and preparation for Christmas.

AMENDMENT - making up for wrong deeds.

ANANIAS - a follower of Jesus who was sent to baptise Paul.

ANDREW - one of the 12, a fisherman and brother of Peter.

ANGEL - pure spiritual beings who worship and serve God continually.

ANNUNCIATION - the announcing to Mary by the Angel Gabriel that she was to be the mother of Jesus.

ANNUNCIATION, FEAST OF - a feast day in the Church on 25 March, 9 months before the Nativity.

ANOINT - to smear or pour oil on the head as a sign that God has specially chosen that person.

ANOINTING OF THE SICK - the sacrament by which a sick, weak or elderly person receives God's strength, peace and healing.

APOCALYPSE - another name for the Book of Revelation, the last book in the Bible.

APOSTLE - *'one sent out'* to preach the good news.

APOSTOLIC - built on the foundation laid by the apostles and continuing their faith in the risen Lord.

ASCEND - to rise up.

ASCENSION - when Jesus was taken up on a cloud to heaven.

ASCENSION THURSDAY - a feast day 10 days before Pentecost Sunday.

ASSEMBLY - gathering.

AUGUSTINE OF CANTERBURY - monk sent by Pope Gregory I to reawaken Christianity in England.

BAPTISM - the first sacrament, the sacrament by which a person becomes a Christian.

BARNABAS - a missionary in the early Church; he gave all he had to the Church *(see Acts 4:36)*.

BARREN - unable to have children.

BARTHOLOMEW - one of the 12 apostles.

BEATIFICATION (BEATIFY) - the stage in the Canonisation process when the Catholic Church recognises a person as 'Blessed' - an exemplary life of holiness.

BEATITUDES - these are eight sayings of Jesus about true happiness with God.

BETHLEHEM - the birth place of Jesus - a little town in Judaea, close to Jerusalem.

BETROTHED - promised in marriage to someone.

BIBLE - the holy book of Christians.

BIBLE REFERENCE - This tells you where to look for a line (or lines) in the Bible.

BIND - to tie up, to make as law.

BISHOP - a leader, teacher and guide for God's People (the Church) in a certain area called a diocese.

BLESSED SACRAMENT - Christ's body, the consecrated host, which is usually reserved (kept safely) in the tabernacle.

BODY OF CHRIST - the way St Paul described the Church.

BONIFACE - an English missionary to Germany and Holland.

CAESAR AUGUSTUS - Roman Emperor at the time of Jesus' birth.

CAIN - Adam and Eve's son; he murdered his brother, Abel.

CANONISATION - the process by which the Catholic Church recognises a person to be a saint.

CANTERBURY - where Augustine and his companions were based in their mission to England in AD 597.

CATACOMBS - underground passages along which the dead of ancient Rome were buried; Christians met there for worship in times of persecution.

CATECHUMEN - a person preparing for Baptism.

CATECHUMENS, OIL OF - the blessed oil with which a person is anointed before they are baptised.

CATECHUMENATE - the period of time in which persons prepare for baptism.

CATHEDRAL - the main church in a diocese.

CATHOLIC - universal, whole.

CENSUS - a count of all people in a particular area.

CHAPTER - each book of the Bible is split into chapters; the chapter number is printed as a bigger number than the verse numbers.

CHARLES LWANGA, St - one of a number of Christian martyrs of Uganda in 1885-87.

CHRISM - a perfumed oil used for anointing.

CHRIST - another word for Messiah; both mean *'Anointed One'* in English.

CHRISTENING - another word for Baptism.

CHRISTIAN FREEDOM - freedom to serve God and others.

CHURCH - the People of God.

CLARE OF ASSISI, St - a young woman who followed St Francis into a life of poverty for love of God; she founded the Poor Clares.

CLEANSE - to clean carefully and thoroughly.

COLUMBA - an Irish missionary to Scotland.

COMMANDMENTS, TEN - the laws God gave to Israel and all people so that they could live at peace with him and in good relations with others.

COMMITMENT - constant effort and enthusiasm for a cause.

COMMUNION - complete union or *'togetherness'*; receiving Christ (Holy Communion) during Mass.

COMMUNION OF SAINTS - the union of the three states of the Church, in heaven, on earth and in purgatory.

COMMUNITY - a group of people who share a common purpose.

CONCEPTION - the first moment of the human being in the womb.

CONFESSION - speaking out sins to God; also a name for the Sacrament of Reconciliation.

CONFESSIONAL - small room in which a person confesses their sins to a priest.

CONFIRMATION - the sacrament by which a person receives the fullness of the Holy Spirit so that they may be mature members of the Church and witnesses for Christ.

CONGREGATION - a gathering of people for worship.

CONSCIENCE - the mind judging freely whether some act is right or wrong.

CONSECRATE - to set aside for a holy purpose.

CONSTANTINE - the Emperor who in AD 313 gave Christians freedom of worship.

CONTRITION - being sorry in your heart for having sinned against God.

CONVERSION - a complete change of heart, turning away from sin and towards God.

CONVOKE - to call together (e.g. a Council of Bishops).

CORNERSTONE - the most important stone in a stone building.

COUNCIL - a gathering of bishops led by the Pope to discuss important matters of Church teaching.

CREED - a summary of what the Church believes about God, Father, Son and Spirit, about the Church and about the things beyond this life.

CROSIER - the long staff carried by a Bishop symbolising his role as a shepherd.

DEANERY - a group of parishes in a diocese.

DECALOGUE - the Ten Commandments.

DESCEND - to come down.

DESPAIR - without hope, hopelessness.

DEVOUT - serving God very faithfully.

DIOCESE - the Church in a certain area for which a bishop is responsible.

DIOCLETIAN - a Roman Emperor who ordered a fierce persecution of the Church in AD 303.

DISCIPLE - *'learner or follower'*; the disciples followed Jesus during his ministry on earth and learnt from him.

DISPENSE - to give out.

DIVINE - of God, Godly.

DIVINE OFFICE - Psalms and prayers said (and sung) daily by members of the Church.

ECCLESIA - Latin word meaning *'assembly'*; it was the word used for *'Church'*.

EFFICACIOUS - effective, having an effect.

ELIZABETH - mother of John the Baptist and a relative of Mary.

ETERNAL - everlasting, never ending.

ETERNAL LIFE - the new life with God given at Baptism.

EUCHARIST - the Sacrament by which Jesus gives himself really, wholly and truly under the appearance of bread and wine.

EVE - the first woman.

EXAMINATION OF CONSCIENCE - looking at my behaviour with God so as to understand my sins and sinful attitudes.

EXORCISM - driving out evil, freeing from the grip of sin.

EXULT - to take delight in someone or something.

FAITH - what is believed to be true about God and the Church.

FIRM PURPOSE OF AMMENDMENT - having a strong wish to do right and avoid wrongdoing in future.

FONT - a special bowl or pool that holds the waters of baptism.

FORGIVENESS - healing a friendship broken by wrongdoing.

FOUND - to set up or establish.

FOUR MARKS OF THE CHURCH - the four marks of the Church are one, holy, catholic and apostolic.

FRANCIS OF ASSISI, St - a well-loved saint born in Italy in 1182; founder of the Franciscans.

GALILEE - a northern Jewish region in which Jesus grew up.

GENESIS - the first book of the Bible.

GENTILE - a person who was not born into the Jewish faith.

GENUFLECT - to go down on the right knee as a sign of reverence before the tabernacle.

GOD'S SELF-REVELATION - how God gradually showed to humans his true nature.

GOSPEL - a word that means 'good news'; there are four Gospels (*of Matthew, Mark, Luke and John*).

GRACE - gift of God's life and help in a person's soul.

GREEK - a very common language in the Roman Empire in the first and second centuries.

HALLOWED - holy.

HANDMAID - a female servant.

HEAVENLY HOST - the angels in heaven around God's throne.

HEBREWS - an early name for the People of Israel.

HEBREW SCRIPTURES - the scriptures of the Jewish faith, the Old Testament to Christians.

HISTORY WRITINGS - the OT books of Israel's history.

HOLY - set apart, Godly.

HOLY FATHER - one of the most common titles for the Pope.

HOLY ORDERS - the sacrament by which a man is made a deacon, priest or bishop so as to serve God's People.

HOLY SOULS - the souls in Purgatory.

HOLY TRINITY - God; Father, Son, and Holy Spirit; three Persons, one God.

HUMILITY - knowing your 'littleness' in the sight of God.

IMMACULATE - without spot or stain.

IMMACULATE CONCEPTION - the teaching that Mary was, from the first moment of her existence, kept free from sin.

IMMACULATE CONCEPTION, FEAST OF - a feast day in the Church on 8 December.

INCARNATION - the teaching that God truly became a man, Jesus, in the womb of Mary; Jesus is truly God and truly man.

INFALLIBLE - without any mistakes.

INITIATION - the way new members of a group are made.

INSPIRATION - the Holy Spirit's guidance and light in the minds of the people who wrote the Bible books.

INSTITUTE - to set up.

INTENTION - the reason, purpose in my mind why I do something.

INTERCEDE - (for) to pray for another person's needs.

INTERCESSION - prayers for the benefit of someone else.

ISRAEL - God's chosen people, the twelve tribes of descendants of Abraham.

JAMES - two of the 12 disciples went by this name; one was the brother of John and a son of Zebedee.

JERUSALEM - the main city in Judea; this is where the Church was born at Pentecost.

JEWS, JEWISH PEOPLE - the name for the people of Israel after about 500 BC.

JOHN - one of the 12 disciples - a young man, he was very close to Jesus; a Gospel and some NT letters come from him.

JOHN THE BAPTIST - a prophet sent to prepare the way for Jesus.

JUDAH/JUDEA - a Jewish region south of Galilee.

JUDAISM - the Jewish Faith.

JUDAS - one of the 12 disciples; he betrayed Jesus by helping the authorities to arrest Jesus.

KEYS TO THE KINGDOM - Jesus gave Simon Peter authority and leadership over the Church, symbolised by 'the keys to the kingdom'.

KING DAVID - the greatest king of ancient Israel.

KINSWOMAN - a female relative.

LAW WRITINGS - the first five books of the OT, also known as the *Torah* or *Pentateuch*.

LECTERN - a stand from which the Bible readings are read during worship.

LETTERS - these are NT writings of St Paul and other apostles to the first Christian groups.

LEVI - another name for Matthew, one of the 12 disciples.

LOOSE - to untie, to cancel a law or rule.

LORD'S PRAYER - the prayer that Jesus taught his disciples, now used by all Christians; also known as the *'Our Father'*.

LOWLY - simple and small.

MAGNIFICAT - Mary's song of praise to God after she had been greeted by Elizabeth.

MANGER - a feeding trough for animals.

MARRIAGE - the sacrament by which a man and woman are made one by God so that they can love each other as husband and wife and be good parents.

MARTYR - a *'witness'*, someone who is willing to stand up for their faith, even if it means death.

MASS - a common name for the celebration of the Eucharist.

MATTHEW - one of the 12 disciples, also known as Levi; a Gospel comes from him.

MAXIMILIAN KOLBE, St - a Polish Franciscan priest who gave his life to save the life of another prisoner.

MEDITATION - silent prayer in the mind.

MESSIAH - also known as the Christ; the leader longed for by the people of Israel; a Hebrew word meaning *'anointed one'*.

MINISTER - a person who serves others in a special way.

MISSIONARY - someone who goes out to preach and teach about Jesus.

MITRE - a bishop's *'hat'*, in the shape of a flame to symbolise the flame of the Spirit that fell on the Apostles.

MORALITY - the goodness or badness of an action.

MORALS - teaching about what is right and wrong, about living as a child of God.

MORAL TEACHING - teaching about right and wrong.

MOSQUE - a place of worship for Muslims.

MUSLIM - a person who follows the beliefs of Islam written in the Qur'an.

MYSTERIES OF THE ROSARY - special times, Joyful, Sorrowful and Glorious, in the lives of Jesus and Mary.

NATIVITY - the birth of Jesus.

NAZARETH - a town in Galilee where Jesus was brought up.

NEOPHYTE - a newly baptised Christian.

NERO - a Roman Emperor who in AD 64 began persecuting Christians in Rome.

NEW TESTAMENT (NT) - the books of the Bible that deal with the life, death and resurrection of Jesus and all that this means for his followers, the Church.

OLD TESTAMENT (OT) - the Jewish books of the Bible; they are about the friendship between God and Israel before the time of Jesus.

ORIGINAL SIN - the sinful tendency that humans inherit from Adam and Eve's disobedience.

PAGAN - one who believes in many gods rather than in one God.

PALESTINE - an area including Galilee and Judea which was taken over by the Roman Empire.

PAPYRUS - an ancient form of paper made from reed fibres.

PARABLE - a simple story with a message to apply to your life.

PARADISE - where Adam and Eve lived in happiness with God.

PARISH - the Church in a small area with a parish church and parish priest.

PARISHIONER - a member of a parish.

PASCHAL CANDLE - the large candle lit at the Easter Vigil Mass.

PASSOVER - a great Jewish festival, celebrating the freedom of the Israelites from slavery under the Egyptians.

PATRICK, St - a missionary and bishop who is called the *'Apostle of Ireland'* for his work in establishing the Christian faith there.

PAUL, St - a man who went from persecuting Jesus' followers to becoming a great leader and missionary in the early Church.

PEACEMAKER - someone who works for peace and spreads peace among others.

PENANCE - something to make up for the damage done by sin; also a name for the Sacrament of Reconciliation.

PENTATEUCH - a name for the first five books of the Bible; these books are also known as the Law or *Torah*.

PENTECOST - a Jewish feast day 50 days after Passover.

PENTECOST SUNDAY - a Christian feast day remembering the Descent of the Holy Spirit upon the apostles and followers of Jesus.

PERPETUA, St - an early Christian martyr; a young mother who refused to give up her Christian faith.

PERPETUAL - never ending.

PERSECUTE - to cause trouble and hurt to others.

PETER (Simon) - Peter was appointed the leader of the 12; Peter means 'rock'.

PETER AND PAUL, SS - a feast day in the Church on 29 June.

PETITION -an 'asking prayer' .

PHARISEE - a Jew at the time of Jesus who kept very closely to Jewish religious law.

PHILIP - one of the 12.

PONDER - to think deeply about something.

POPE - a word meaning 'father'; used for the Bishop of Rome, believed by Catholics to be the Head of the Church on earth.

PRAYER OF INTERCESSION - asking for help from God for someone else.

PRAYER OF PETITION - asking for help from God.

PREACH - to speak out, to proclaim (e.g. the Word of God).

PRESENTATION - when Jesus, 40 days after his birth, was presented in the Temple in obedience to Jewish religious law.

PRIDE - a wish to live without God and to think yourself the best.

PROCLAIM - to speak out or to announce (important news).

PRODIGAL - wasteful.

PROPHECY - The OT books in which a prophet hears God's message and is sent to the people to speak it out.

PROVERB - a wise saying that is easy to remember.

PSALMS - beautiful songs/poems to God collected into a book of the Bible.

PURGATORY - the experience of being purified (made clean) for God after death.

RCIA - Rite of Christian Initiation of Adults; a way of bringing older people into the Church.

RECONCILIATION - mending a broken friendship; a sacrament by which a person who is truly sorry receives the forgiveness of Jesus through a priest (also called *Confession*, *Penance*).

REMORSE - feeling bad after doing wrong.

REPENTANCE - turning to God and being truly sorry.

RESPONSIBILITY - thinking about the results of my actions; being trustworthy.

REVELATION - the way God slowly but surely showed himself to Israel by his Word; Christians believe that Jesus is God's full self-revelation.

REVELATION, BOOK OF - The last book of the Bible, also known as Apocalypse.

RITE - the order and way in which a sacrament is celebrated.

ROMAN EMPIRE - the great area of land and seas ruled by the Romans; it stretched from England to Asia at its height.

ROSARY - a prayer in which the *'Our Father'*, *'Hail Mary'*, *'Glory Be'* are said prayerfully many times.

ROSARY BEADS - beads that help to count prayers said so that the person praying can think about praying rather than numbers.

SACRAMENT - a living sign by which we receive God's help for our souls in a particular way.

SACRAMENTS OF HEALING - sacraments to bring peace and wholeness in mind and body - Reconciliation and the Anointing of the Sick.

SACRAMENTS OF INITIATION - sacraments by which a person is drawn into full membership of the Church - Baptism, Confirmation and Eucharist.

SACRAMENTS OF MINISTRY - sacraments by which a person receives grace for a special role of service - Marriage, Holy Orders.

SACRED SCRIPTURE - another name for the Bible.

SACRED TRADITION - the teaching of the Apostles about Christ passed down to the Church through the ages.

SALVATION - being saved, being completely close to God.

SAUL - another name for St Paul.

SAINT - a word meaning 'holy'; a saint grows to complete love of God and their neighbour.

SCAPEGOAT - someone who takes the blame even when it's not their fault.

SERENITY - peace inside yourself.

SERVANT OF THE SERVANTS OF GOD - one of the titles for the Pope.

SHEEPFOLD - a fenced area for sheep; it also was used as an image of the Church.

SIGN - something that gets across a message.

SIGNIFY - to be a sign of.

SIMEON - a faithful believer in God who held the baby Jesus in his arms, knowing that he was the Messiah, the Promised One.

SIMON - two of the 12 disciples were called this name.

SIN - an offence against God, failing to love.

SPOKEN PRAYER - prayer using words.

STATE OF GRACE - God being *'at home'* in my soul, having God's life in me.

SUCCESSOR - someone who follows in the footsteps of another, who takes on that person's duties and responsibilities.

SUPERNATURAL - above ordinary life, the spiritual life with God.

SWADDLING CLOTHES - warm strips of cloth wrapped around a baby.

SYMBOL - something simple that leads one to imagine a bigger, more mysterious reality.

SYMBOLISE - to be a symbol of.

SYMBOLIC GESTURE - a special movement of hand or body, a movement that means something.

SYMBOLIC STORY - a story that uses symbols to get across important truths.

TABERNACLE - place in a church where Christ's body, the consecrated hosts, is held for worship and adoration.

TAX COLLECTOR - one who collected tax for the Romans from the Jews; tax collectors were usually hated and considered to be sinners.

TEMPLE - Jewish place of worship and sacrifice in Jerusalem; it was destroyed in 70 AD by the Romans.

TEMPTATION - thoughts that lead us to sin if we follow through on them.

TEN COMMANDMENTS - ten rules for living life to the full given by God through Moses to Israel.

TESTAMENT - a solemn friendship agreement between God and his People.

THADDAEUS - one of the 12 disciples.

THANKSGIVING - prayer in which thanks is offered to God for all his good gifts.

THOMAS - one of the 12 disciples.

TORAH - a name for the first five books of the Bible; these books are also known as the Law or Pentateuch.

TRESPASSES - sins, offences.

TRUST - belief in a person's goodness towards you.

UNITY - being together, being one in heart and mind.

VATICAN - a tiny State in Rome where the Pope and many organisations of the Catholic Church are based.

VENERABLE - title given to someone at an early stage of being recognised as a saint (canonised).

VERSE - the smallest part, usually a line or two, into which a Bible book is split.

VICAR - someone who acts officially in the place of someone else.

VICAR OF CHRIST - one of the titles for the Pope.

VISITATION - Mary's visit to Elizabeth after she had been told the news by the Angel Gabriel.

VOCATION - a calling, a direction in life a person receives from God.

WHITSUN - another name for Pentecost Sunday.

WISDOM WRITINGS - these OT books are about how to live wisely and well in the sight of God and other people.

ZACCHAEUS - a chief tax collector who repented after meeting Jesus.

ZECHARIAH - father of John the Baptist and husband of Elizabeth.